Dr Devdutt Pattanaik is a medical doctor by training, a marketing manager by profession and a mythologist by passion. He topped the Mumbai University course in Comparative Mythology and lectures extensively on the relevance of sacred stories, symbols and rituals in modern times. His books include *Shiva: An Introduction* (VFS, India), *Vishnu: An Introduction* (VFS, India), *Devi: An Introduction* (VFS, India), *Hanuman: An Introduction* (VFS, India), *Lakshmi:An Introduction* (VFS, India), *Krishna: An Introduction* (VFS, India), *Shiva to Shankara:Decoding the Phallic Symbol* (Indus Source, India), *Goddesses in India* (Inner Traditions, USA), *Man Who Was a Woman and Other Queer Tales from Hindu Lore* (Harrington Press, USA) and *Indian Mythology: Stories, Symbols and Rituals from the Heart of the Subcontinent* (Inner Traditions, USA). *The Book of Kali* (Penguin, India) is based on his lectures.

PRAISE FOR THE BOOK

'At last we have a brilliant pocket-sized handbook on Hindu mythology written in English by an Indian . . . Divided—like the holy trinity—into three chapters (dedicated to Brahma–Saraswati, Vishnu–Lakshmi and Shiva–Shakti), the book delves into virtually every important myth and story associated with these gods/goddesses (and their progeny, associates and antagonists) in simple and engaging prose that draws from a host of original and secondary sources from the Vedas to the Puranas. Indeed, in Pattanaik, Indian civilization has found an articulator of the calibre of Will Durant'—*India Today*

'Hitch-hikers, here's your guide to the Hindu multiverse and all the thirty-three million deities. Mythology demystified but not dumbed down. Delves for the *sat* behind the *mithya*, and isn't heavy-handed or maudlin about it; there's real affection in these retellings'—*Tehelka*

'Who doesn't love a good story? Devdutt Pattanaik knows that it's a human weakness [and] his *Myth=Mithya* tells lots of the glorious stories that make Hinduism so endlessly fascinating'—*Time Out Mumbai*

'"A Handbook of Hindu Mythology", the cover reads. But this book is all that and much, much more . . . stories as varied as those from the *Rig Veda*, *Ramayana*, the

Skanda Purana, and folklore haven't been written with such simplicity, economy of words, even humour . . . Recommended to every kind of reader—uninitiated or expert—with an interest in mythology. Read it just for the relish of wonderfully told stories (and the sheer variety of sources), [even] if you dislike analysing your myths too much' —*First City*

Myth=Mithya

A Handbook of Hindu Mythology

DR DEVDUTT PATTANAIK

Illustrations by the Author

PENGUIN BOOKS

PENGUIN BOOKS
Published by the Penguin Group
Penguin Books India Pvt. Ltd, 11 Community Centre, Panchsheel Park,
New Delhi 110 017, India
Penguin Group (USA) Inc., 375 Hudson Street, New York, New York 10014,
USA
Penguin Group (Canada), 90 Eglinton Avenue East, Suite 700, Toronto,
Ontario, M4P 2Y3, Canada (a division of Pearson Penguin Canada Inc.)
Penguin Books Ltd, 80 Strand, London WC2R 0RL, England
Penguin Ireland, 25 St Stephen's Green, Dublin 2, Ireland (a division of Penguin
Books Ltd)
Penguin Group (Australia), 250 Camberwell Road, Camberwell, Victoria
3124, Australia (a division of Pearson Australia Group Pty Ltd)
Penguin Group (NZ), 67 Apollo Drive, Rosedale, Auckland 0632,
New Zealand (a division of Pearson New Zealand Ltd)
Penguin Group (South Africa) (Pty) Ltd, 24 Sturdee Avenue, Rosebank,
Johannesburg 2196, South Africa

Penguin Books Ltd, Registered Offices: 80 Strand, London WC2R 0RL,
England

First published by Penguin Books India 2006

Text and illustrations copyright © Devdutt Pattanaik 2006

All rights reserved

23 22 21 20 19

ISBN 9780143099703

For sale in the Indian Subcontinent and Singapore only

Typeset in Perpetua by Eleven Arts, New Delhi
Printed at Anubha Printers, Noida

Contents

Author's Note

- The stories in this book are my own retellings, often simplified with a great deal of poetic licence, to accommodate—without losing the essence—details from various versions of the same story found in different scriptures
- No italics have been used to distinguish between English and non-English words
- Capital letters have been restricted to names and titles except where explicitly stated
- 'Gods' and 'Goddesses' spelt with an initial capital letter need to be distinguished from 'gods' and 'goddesses' in lowercase. The former are manifestations of the infinite divine while the latter are finite forms of the divine. Shiva is God but Indra is god. Durga is Goddess but Ganga is goddess.
- Sanskrit words are sometimes used as proper nouns and begin with a capital letter (for example, Maya, the Goddess who embodies delusion) and sometimes as common nouns spelt without capitals (for example, maya, delusion)
- This handbook is *a* decoding of Hindu mythology, firm in the belief that:

> Within infinite myths lies the eternal truth,
> Who sees it all?
> Varuna has but a thousand eyes
> Indra a hundred
> And I, only two.

How to Read This Book:
Author's Recommendation

You don't have to go through this book sequentially. While that helps, you can also choose to dip into the book at random and read the captions under the illustrations and the tables and flowcharts. If you do decide to read it sequentially, do so at a leisurely pace. Take time to absorb and enjoy the ideas before you move on.

Introduction: Myth=Mithya

*In which the meaning of myth, its value
and expression are elaborated*

Everybody lives in myth. This idea disturbs most people. For conventionally myth means falsehood. Nobody likes to live in falsehood. Everybody believes they live in truth.

But there are many types of truth. Some objective, some subjective. Some logical, some intuitive. Some cultural, some universal. Some are based on evidence; others depend on faith. Myth is truth which is subjective, intuitive, cultural and grounded in faith.

Ancient Greek philosophers knew myth as mythos. They distinguished mythos from logos. From mythos came intuitive narrations, from logos reasonable deliberations. Mythos gave rise to the oracles and the arts. From logos came science and mathematics. Logos explained how the sun rises and how babies are born. It took man to the moon. But it never explained why. Why does the sun rise? Why is a baby born? Why does man exist on earth? For answers one had to turn to mythos. Mythos gave purpose, meaning and validation to existence.

Ancient Hindu seers knew myth as mithya. They distinguished mithya from sat. Mithya was truth seen through a frame of reference. Sat was truth independent of any frame of reference. Mithya gave a limited, distorted view of reality; sat a limitless, correct view of things. Mithya was delusion, open to correction.

Sat was truth, absolute and perfect in every way. Being boundless and perfect, however, sat could not be reduced to a symbol or confined to a word. Words and symbols are essentially incomplete and flawed. Sat therefore eluded communication. For communication one needs symbols and words, howsoever incomplete and flawed they may be. Through hundreds of thousands of incomplete and flawed symbols and words, it was possible to capture, or at least to indicate, the infinite perfection and boundlessness of sat. For Rishis therefore the delusion of mithya served as an essential window to the truth of sat.

Myth is essentially a cultural construct, a common understanding of the world that binds individuals and communities together. This understanding may be religious or secular. Ideas such as rebirth, heaven and hell, angels and demons, fate and freewill, sin, Satan and salvation are religious myths. Ideas such as sovereignty, nation state, human rights, women's rights, animal rights and gay rights are secular myths. Religious or secular, all myths make profound sense to one group of people. Not to everyone. They cannot be rationalized beyond a point. In the final analysis, you either accept them or you don't.

If myth is an idea, mythology is the vehicle of that idea. Mythology constitutes stories, symbols and rituals that make a myth tangible. Stories, symbols and rituals are essentially languages—languages that are heard, seen and performed. Together they construct the truths of a culture. The story of the Resurrection, the symbol of the crucifix and the ritual of baptism establish the idea that is

Christianity. The story of independence, the symbol of the national flag and the ritual of the national anthem reinforce the idea of a nation state.

Mythology tends to be hyperbolic and fantastic to drive home a myth. It is modern arrogance to presume that in ancient times people actually believed in the objective existence of virgin births, flying horses, parting seas, talking serpents, gods with six heads and demons with eight arms. The sacredness of such obviously irrational plots and characters ensures their flawless transmission over generations. Any attempt to challenge their validity is met with outrage. Any attempt to edit them is frowned upon. The unrealistic content draws attention to the idea behind the communication. Behind virgin births and parting seas is an entity who is greater than all forces of nature put together. A god with six heads and a demon with eight arms project a universe where there are infinite possibilities, for the better and for the worse.

From myth come beliefs, from mythology customs. Myth conditions thoughts and feelings. Mythology influences behaviours and communications. Myth and mythology thus have a profound influence on culture. Likewise, culture has a profound influence on myth and mythology. People outgrow myth and mythology when myth and mythology fail to respond to their cultural needs. So long as Egyptians believed in the afterworld ruled by Osiris, they built pyramids. So long as Greeks believed in Charon, the ferryman of the dead, they placed copper coins for him in the mouth of the dead. Today no one believes in Osiris or Charon. There are no pyramids or coins in the mouth of the dead. Instead there are new funeral ceremonies spawned by new belief systems, new mythologies based on new myths, each one helping people cope with the painful inevitability and mystery of death.

It is ironical that for all the value we give to the rational, life is primarily governed by the irrational. Love is not rational. Sorrow is not rational. Hatred, ambition, rage and greed are irrational. Even ethics, morals and aesthetics are not rational. They depend on values and standards which are ultimately subjective. What is right, sacred and beautiful to one group of people need not be right, sacred and beautiful to another group of people. Every opinion and every decision depends on the prevailing myth. Even perfection is a myth. There is no evidence of a perfect world, a perfect man or a perfect family anywhere on earth. Perfection, be it Rama Rajya or Camelot, exists only in mythology. Yet everyone craves for it. This craving inspires art, establishes empires, sparks revolutions and motivates leaders. Such is the power of myth.

This book explores Hindu mythology. Behind the mythology is a myth. Behind the myth a truth: an inherited truth about life and death, about nature and culture, about perfection and possibility, about hierarchies and horizons. This subjective and cultural truth of the Hindus is neither superior nor inferior to other truths. It is simply yet another human understanding of life.

1
The Circle of Brahma and Saraswati

In which the nature of the universe is explored

The circle is the most spontaneous of natural shapes, taken by the horizon, by stars, planets and bubbles. It best represents the Hindu universe because Hindus see the world as being timeless, fetterless, boundless, cyclical and infinite. This universe is the medium through which the divine presents itself; hence for Hindus every element of this universe can serve as a window to the divine.

Brahma

God as creator looks like a priest, chanting Vedic hymns and holding in his four hands instruments of ritual. Every ritual is concluded with the chant 'Shanti, shanti, shanti', which means 'Peace, peace, peace'. Peace is the aim of every ritual. Peace comes when one comes to terms with the three worlds: the personal world, the cultural world and the natural world. For that one needs to appreciate the world in its totality, from every point of view. That is what Brahma does with his four heads facing the four directions.

For Hindus, Brahma is God who creates the world. The world he creates is known as Brahmanda. This world is not just the outer objective world governed by mathematical principles. It is also the inner subjective world of thoughts and feelings. According to Vedic scriptures, God does not 'create' this world. He simply made all creatures aware of it. Awareness leads to discovery. Discovery is creation.

The world discovered by Brahma is embodied in the Goddess. She has always existed, even when no one observed her. For Brahma, the Goddess is Shatarupa, she who takes infinite forms.

Shatarupa is Saraswati, goddess of knowledge, for in her infinite forms she reflects the answer to Brahma's question: Who am I? This question is the impulse of creation. It made God open his eyes and look at the Goddess.

Saraswati

Saraswati is Goddess as embodiment of knowledge. She is the world that informs and inspires. She wears no jewels or cosmetics and drapes herself in a plain white sari with no desire to allure. She must be sought out. She rides a heron, the symbol of concentration, or a gander, the symbol of intellectual discrimination because it is believed to possess the ability to separate water and milk from a mixture. She holds in her four hands a lute, a book, a pen and a string of memory beads. Difficult to acquire yet eternally faithful, she is the container of all answers.

Three Hundred and Thirty Million Deities

Here we uncover the layers of divine manifestations and understand the relationships between them.

The idea of 330 million Hindu deities is a metaphor for the countless forms by which the divine makes itself accessible to the human mind.

Vishwa-rupa

Vishwa-rupa or Virat-Swarup is the cosmic form of God. For Hindus, God is the container of all things. All existence is a manifestation of the divine. This understanding of the world makes no room for the notion of 'evil'. Evil means that which is devoid of Godliness. When everything is God, then nothing, not even things we despise and shy away from, can be ungodly. Good and bad are judgements based on human values. Human values—critical though they may be to establishing civilized society—are based on a limited understanding of the world. When understanding changes, values and judgements change and with them society. The Sanskrit word 'maya' refers to all things that can be measured. Human understanding of the world is limited, hence measurable, hence maya. To believe this maya is truth is delusion. Beyond maya, beyond human values and human judgements, beyond the current understanding of the world, is a limitless reality which makes room for everyone and everything. That reality is God.

For Hindus, all of creation is divine. Everything in nature is therefore worthy of worship. There is no discomfort visualizing God in plants, animals, rivers, mountains, rocks and in man-made objects such as pots, pans, pestles and mortars. Stories such as the one following transform rivers into molten forms of God.

Vishnu Melts

God creates the world as Brahma, sustains it as Vishnu and destroys it as Shiva. One day, Shiva started to sing. Vishnu was so moved by the melody that he began to melt. Brahma caught the molten Vishnu in a pot. This was poured on earth. It took the form of the river Ganga. The Ganga nourished the earth. To bathe in Ganga's waters is to bathe in God. (Ganga Mahatmya)

A Hindu deity may be just a rock in a cave, a tree growing in an orchard, a river flowing down the plains, a cow wandering in the street, or perhaps an elaborately decorated idol of stone, clay or metal enshrined in a temple. Anything can be God. So long as it can respond to the human condition. In many shrines, deities are given human form merely by placing a pair of eyes and a pair of hands on a rock. Eyes represent sense organs and hands represent action organs. This indicates the deity is conscious, sensitive and responsive.

Grama-devi

A village goddess or Grama-devi is characterized by her eyes, indicating she is sensitive to the needs of her worshippers. With an upward-pointing palm, the goddess offers emotional comfort. With a downward-pointing palm, the goddess offers material gifts. Her nose ring and bangles are a reminder that the goddess is domesticated: her power has been harnessed for the benefit of the village.

Divine sensitivity and responsiveness vary from place to place. Certain natural rock formations are found to be more potent than others. This explains why a particular set of three stones in a cave in Jammu attracts hundreds of pilgrims who identify them as the tangible manifestation of the Goddess, locally known as

Vaishno-devi. Or why a particular icicle in a remote, inaccessible Himalayan cave is identified with Shiva and revered as Amarnath, the eternal lord.

Divine potency can also be a function of time. The confluence of the Ganga and the Yamuna is for Hindus more sacred than the confluence of any other rivers. Hence more pilgrims bathe at this sangam. The flow of pilgrims rises dramatically when the planet Jupiter enters the house of Aries, and the sun enters the house of Capricorn. This planetary alignment takes place once in twelve years, which is marked by the Maha Kumbha Mela, the great gathering of holy men, believed to be the largest religious congregation in the world.

It is possible, through certain prescribed rituals, to transform an idol into a deity, make an ordinary object of art sensitive and responsive to the human condition. In such images divine aura wanes over time, with more and more people seeking its darshan. Regular rituals performed by well-trained priests ensure the aura is replenished. To minimize loss of aura, the image is isolated in the sanctum sanctorum, a room which is rather dark, cramped and off limits to the public. Only priests who have been ritually cleansed are allowed to enter the room and touch the idol. Devotees can look upon the image from afar and that too for not more than a few minutes. Once or twice a year, during festivals, the deity or its effigy leaves the temple in a grand procession to mingle freely with the people.

For Hindus, looking at the image of God is important. This ritual act is known as darshan. During darshan the deity looks at your condition and responds to it. Thus darshan draws the transformative power of God into one's life. Devotees of Shrinathji suffer long waits for hours in the crowded halls of his haveli in Nathdvara, Rajasthan, even though his darshan lasts for barely a few seconds, which is why it is locally known as jhanki or a teasing glimpse.

Turning for Kanakadasa

The image of Krishna in the temple at Udipi used to face the east. Only high-caste people were allowed to enter this temple. Kanakadasa, a low-caste devotee, stood outside near the western wall, desperate to catch a glimpse of the lord. To everyone's surprise, the image in the sanctum turned west, allowing Kanakadasa to see him through a crack in the western wall. (Udipi temple lore)

Some images are svayambhu, naturally potent, hence attract throngs of devotees. They need few, if any, aura-replenishing rituals. Balaji, the deity who resides atop the hills of Tirumala, Andhra Pradesh, is said to be so sensitive to people's needs that even though his eyes are covered with sandal paste he is able to respond to the needs of over a hundred thousand pilgrims who visit his temple every day.

As devotees leave a shrine, they try to carry with them anything that has come in contact with the deity: dry flakes of sandal paste, ash, water, flowers, cloth or food. This is prasad. It contains divine aura by coming in contact with God. It has the power to carry divine blessings wherever it goes. The principle underlying this practice is called 'contagious magic', the ability to transmit sacredness through contact.

Nandini's Milk

Many temples claim that the images they enshrine are not carved by human hands. They are said to have been found in a termite hill by cowherds who found their cows shedding milk over it. Such tales transform the images into svayambhu svarupas, self-created images of a very conscious God, who wants to be found.

A deity may be worshipped in a temporary open-air shrine made of bamboo, cane and cloth that is dismantled after the ceremony. Or it may be placed in a permanent shrine: inside the house, restricted to the family, or in a public space, open to the community. A Hindu temple is not a prayer hall or the space where the faithful gather; it is the residence of God. Each day the presiding deity is bathed, fed, bedecked and adored. Each day the deity grants audience to devotees, accepting their offerings and answering their prayers.

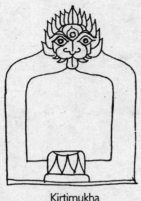

Kirtimukha

This rather fierce-looking head with tongue sticking out often adorns doorways and arches of temples. Its irreverent, mocking expression contrasts with the serenity of the presiding deity. It reminds everyone that God can see beyond the piety being expressed. The unspoken truths in the hearts of the devotees are not hidden from God.

For Hindus, the temple is as important as the deity within. The deity gives meaning to the temple; if the deity did not exist, the devotees would not go to the temple. If the temple did not exist, if there were no magnificent archways, embellished walls, decorated roofs or fluttering flags, devotees would not know where to look for the deity. Thus the temple and the deity within validate each other. The temple is the body and the deity, its soul.

Hindu temple walls are covered with all kinds of images, both real and imagined. There are scenes from everyday life: priests performing yagna, kings fighting battles, warriors hunting, courtesans dancing, couples making love, children playing and sages giving discourse. Then there are fantastic forms: gods with

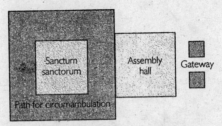

Elements of a Hindu Temple

multiple heads, goddesses with many arms, demons with fangs, mythical beasts—part serpent, part lion, part elephant. The sacred and the profane, the sexual and the violent, the factual and the fictional, the desired and the disgusting merge and mingle with each other. Hindu temple art informs the viewer that everything can and does exist in the world. There can be no limits to God. Hence Brahmanda is boundless, the possibilities within endless. Hindu temples are thus architectural expressions of the Hindu understanding of the world.

Narasimha

Narasimha is a form of Vishnu that is neither man nor animal. It is neither this nor that. For many, this is a monster because it cannot be classified. For the devotee, this is God, because it defies classification. Images such as these which emerge from beyond the limits of human vision and vocabulary embellish Hindu temple walls. They remind all that what is impossible in human reason is possible in divine thought.

In the earliest phase of Hinduism, known as the Vedic age, there were no temples. The need for permanent shrines came much later when the nomadic lifestyle gave way to a more settled agricultural life. Temple or no temple, the aim of invoking the divine in all phases of Hinduism has been the same: to cope with the stress of existence. The response took, and continues to take, three forms:

1. Fight: rites and rituals aimed at changing circumstances in one's favour
2. Flight: monastic ideologies that sought an alternative, less tumultuous reality
3. Freeze: submission to a higher power who then guides one's destiny

The ritual known as yagna was the cornerstone of religious activity in Vedic times. Priests, on behalf of a patron, sat around a fire altar, chanted hymns and made offerings of milk and butter into the flames, invoking celestial beings known as Devas and compelling them by the power of ritual to satisfy the material aspirations of the patron. Pleased with the chants and offerings, the Devas gave victory in battle, brought rains on time and gave children to the childless.

Table Three Phases of Hinduism

Phase of Hinduism	Characteristic Feature	Approximate Dating
Age of Rituals (Karma Kanda)	Focus on execution of rituals that realizes desire or changes destiny (highly mechanical)	1500 BC to 500 BC (Vedic era)
Age of Speculation (Gyan Kanda)	Focus on a deeper understanding of desire and destiny (highly intellectual)	500 BC to AD 500 (Upanishadic era)
Age of Worship (Upasana Kanda)	Focus on appeasement and adoration of deities whose grace can realize desire or change destiny (highly emotional)	AD 500 to present times (Bhakti era)

Dasharatha's Sons

Dasharatha had three wives but no sons. So he invited Rishi Rishyashringamuni to perform a yagna. At the end of the yagna, a Deva appeared from the flames and gave Dasharatha a pot of sweet porridge. 'Give it to your wife and she will bear a son,' said the Deva. Dasharatha gave half the porridge to his senior queen, Kaushalya, and half to his favourite queen, Kaikeyi. Both queens gave half of their share to the youngest queen, Sumitra. As a result Kaushalya gave birth to Rama, Kaikeyi to Bharata and Sumitra to the twins Lakshmana and Shatrughna. Rama and Lakshmana were inseparable, as were Bharata and Shatrughna. (Ramayana)

Vedic gods resided above the earth. There was Agni, fire, who stood on the ground. There was Vayu, wind, who extended between earth and sky. There was Indra, who ruled the sky and brought rain by attacking monsoon clouds with his thunderbolt. Then came Surya, the sun, Chandra, the moon, and seven other celestial bodies or Grahas whose movements across the twelve solar houses and twenty-seven lunar houses aroused great curiosity. Not only did they indicate the change of seasons, they also mapped out the destiny of man. It was in Vedic times that Jyotisha-shastra or astrology came into being. It enabled man to distinguish favourable times from unfavourable times. It foretold future calamities and provided the means to realize dreams or modify destiny using the power of gemstones and rituals that realigned the power of the Grahas.

Chandra

Like all celestial bodies, Chandra, the moon-god, travels through the twelve solar houses, the Rashis, and the twenty-seven lunar houses, the Nakshatras. The Nakshatras are said to be the wives of the moon. His favourite Nakshatra is Rohini. He waxes as he moves towards her and wanes as he moves away from her. On the twenty-eighth day, when there is no wife next to Chandra, the sky is dark, with no trace of the moon. On this day the moon sits on Shiva's head. The story goes that he was so handsome that Tara, the star-goddess, wife of Brihaspati, Jupiter, eloped with him. The child thus conceived was Budh, Mercury. Indra, king of the sky, decreed though the child was fathered by the moon its legitimate father was Brihaspati.

The list of astrological deities includes not only Devas but also Rishis (Brihaspati and Shukra) and Asuras (Rahu and Ketu). Rishis were keepers of Vedic lore and, in Vedic times, those who possessed a deep understanding of this highly revered scripture were considered as powerful as the gods. Asuras were enemies of the Devas; they resided under the earth. Though Asuras, Rahu and Ketu were special. They lived in the skies as eclipses and comets influencing the design of the celestial regions and hence

Table   The Gods of Time

Name of Deity	Celestial Body	Associated Mental State	Associated Animal	Associated Mineral
Surya	Sun	Leadership	Horse	Ruby
Chandra	Moon	Mood swings	Antelope	Pearl
Mangal	Mars	Aggressiveness	Lion	Coral
Budh	Mercury	Intelligence	Lion with an elephant's trunk	Emerald
Brihaspati	Jupiter	Rationality	Elephant	Yellow sapphire
Shukra	Venus	Creativity	Horse	Diamond
Shani	Saturn	Impatience	Vulture	Blue sapphire
Rahu	Eclipse	Confusion	Serpent's head	Hessonite
Ketu	Comet	Restlessness	Serpent's tail	Cat's eye

influencing the destiny of those on earth. Rahu and Ketu therefore became worthy of worship, to be appeased rather than adored. The following story explains how Rahu and Ketu came to sit alongside the gods.

Rahu and Ketu

Once the Adityas and Daityas, sons of Aditi and Diti by the sage Kashyapa, were fighting over a pot of Amrita, the nectar of immortality. Vishnu, who is God, took the enchanting female form of Mohini and offered to distribute it between them. Smitten by her beauty, both sets of half-brothers accepted the offer. Distracting the Daityas with her alluring smile, Mohini poured Amrita down the throats of the Adityas. One Daitya got suspicious. He went and sat among the Adityas. As the Amrita fell into his mouth, the sun and the moon recognized the intruder. They alerted Vishnu, who immediately hurled his discus and severed the Daitya's neck. The head became the demon Rahu, who swore to eclipse the sun and the moon from time to time. The body became the demon Ketu, a directionless comet. Since the Daityas did not get a drop of Amrita, they became known as Asuras, those who did not drink the divine nectar. The Adityas became known as Suras, those who did drink the divine nectar. The Suras were Devas, or gods of light, illuminated by Amrita. (Mahabharata)

Rahu is represented as having a serpent's head while Ketu has a serpent's tail. Nagas or hooded serpents have a close relationship with Asuras. Both live under the earth. Both crave for Amrita that the Devas jealously guard. Both are associated with the idea of renewal. Deprived of Amrita, the Asuras take the help of Shukra, Venus, their guru, who has knowledge of Sanjivani Vidya, which allows him to resurrect dead Asuras. Nagas possess the power to regenerate themselves, replace their old skin with new ones because they had slithered on the grass where the pot of Amrita was once kept. This ability to be reborn, renewed and resurrected has made the Asuras and Nagas earth-bound deities. They are associated with fertility rites, and invoked for children and harvest.

Naga

Serpents are symbols of change and renewal. Like the earth they renew their fertility by replacing old skin with new. Since they could slither above and below the earth, they were considered keepers of the earth's secrets and hence symbols of occult lore. Serpents reminded Rishis of rivers meandering through the plains. They become symbols of life and time that keeps moving in one direction. Hindu deities are commonly associated with serpents. Shiva, the ascetic form of God, lets a serpent sit on him, while Vishnu, the royal form of God, sits on top of a serpent. This is because Shiva merely witnesses the earth's fertile rhythms while Vishnu controls it to establish society. The Goddess holds the serpent in her hand. She is the serpent—the earth, the river, time and life—that Shiva and Vishnu respond to.

The Vedic age also saw the writing of Vastu-shastra, a treatise that compiled methods of manipulating the forces of space. Attention was given to the Diggapalas, guardians of the four cardinal and four ordinal directions. By placing doors, windows, walls and water tanks in various directions, it was possible to enrich a dwelling and make fortune flow in a particular direction. An analysis of the locations of the Diggapalas shows a great need for balance. Indra, god of freshwater rains, sits on the east,

North-west = Vayu = wind-god	North = Kubera = god of growth	North-east = Chandra = moon-god
West = Varuna = god of sea water		East = Indra = god of rain-water
South-west = Surya = sun-god	South = Yama = god of decay	South-east = Agni = fire-god

The Guardians of Space

balanced by Varuna, god of sea water, sitting in the west. The moon sits in the north-east, balancing the sun, who sits in the south-west. The fire-god sits in the south-east, balancing the wind-god, who sits in the north-west. In the south sits Yama, god of death and decay, balanced by Kubera, god of treasures and growth, guardian of the north.

Kubera is neither Deva nor Asura nor Naga nor Rishi. He is a Yaksha. This class of beings is associated with water, metals and gems. These being were visualized as fat, misshapen creatures who lived in uninhabited forests close to waterbodies. They could be both malevolent and benevolent. They are hoarders of wealth. Kubera, king of the Yakshas, lives in the city of Alakapuri in the north. He is the treasurer of the Devas.

Kubera

Fat and dwarfish Kubera, king of the Yakshas, is the treasurer of the Devas. He is the guardian of treasures. His pet mongoose spits out precious gems. Unlike other gods who travel on animals and birds, he travels on the backs of human beings. He represents the earth's hidden wealth that everyone craves for.

The inclusion of earth-bound gods such as Asuras, Nagas and Yakshas in the pantheon of Vedic gods is a clear indicator that, with the passage of time, the sky-gazing nomads were becoming increasingly drawn to the mysteries of the earth. As lifestyle became more settled and less nomadic, the ritual of yagna was abandoned or abbreviated in favour of the puja.

With the puja came a slightly different approach to the divine. The gods were no longer compelled to do man's bidding; they were appeased or adored and their grace sought with offerings of food, flowers, clothes, jewels, incense and lamps. Though the method changed, the intention was the same: to realize desires or change destiny—or to make a request to obtain the strength to cope with life.

Puja makes gods more personal. There are Ishta-devatas or personal gods, Kula-devatas or family gods, Graha-devatas or household gods, and Grama-devatas or village gods. These gods either protected their worshippers or provided for them.

Protector or guardian gods are usually male. Known as viras, or brave ones, they are visualized as mustachioed hypermasculine men who ride horses, brandish swords and spears, kill demons and have the virility to pleasure many wives. Their images are typically placed at the frontiers of villages, keeping out the malevolent forces of the forests that threaten the settlement. Ayyanar is a popular guardian god of the South while Khandoba is well known in the Deccan Plateau.

Khandoba

The folk guardian god of the Maratha community. Like all such guardian gods, Khandoba sports a moustache, rides a white horse and swings a sword. He is identified with Shiva.

Provider or fertility gods are usually female. Known as matas, or mothers, they are usually represented by a pair of eyes and hands placed on a vermilion-smeared rock. The body of the goddess is composed of the houses, the fields and the pasturelands of the village. She in effect sustains the entire community with her fertility. To draw her resources, the villagers have domesticated her fertility and controlled her procreative powers. They have fenced her, pulled out the weeds and decided which seed should be germinated in her soil. But once a year, the wild, untamed form of the goddess is unleashed. On this the goddess reclaims her fertility by demanding blood sacrifices. By quenching her thirst with blood she is able to replenish her spent energy and nurture the community for the rest of the year. Villages are often named after the village goddess; for example, Tuljapur in Maharashtra is named after

Mata Tulja Bhavani and Chandigarh is named after Mansa Chandi Devi. The city of Mumbai encloses within its urban sprawl several villages, hence has several Grama-devi shrines, the most popular of which is Mumba-devi.

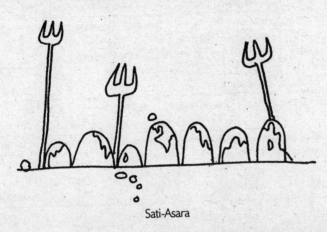

Sati-Asara

Seven rocks representing seven virgins or seven mothers are found in many parts of India. Found next to rivers or ponds or lakes, under the shade of neem or tamarind or lemon trees, they are worshipped mainly by women seeking children. The seven rocks are never kept in a temple or served by a priest. They are identified merely by the vermilion powder they are smeared with.

While the Age of Rituals focused on the yagna and the Age of Worship focused on the puja, the Age of Speculation, which connected the two periods, had brought to the attention of the Hindus complex metaphysical ideas such as the immortal soul and the web of karma. These speculations provided a deeper understanding of life. There was more to existence than realizing desires and following destiny. While Devas, Asuras, Nagas, Yaskhas

Table The Hierarchy of the Divine

Nirguna Brahman = Divine without form						
Saguna Brahman = Divine with form						
Purusha = Bhagavan = Divine within = Spiritual reality = God				Prakriti = Bhagavati = Divine without = Material reality = Goddess		
Brahma = creator	Vishnu = preserver, affirmer	Shiva = destroyer, renouncer	Saraswati = knowledge	Lakshmi = wealth	Shakti = power	
	Incarnations of Vishnu	Sons of Shiva			Kali = wild	Gauri = domestic
Diggapalas = gods of space	Grahas = gods of time		Devas = sky gods	Asuras/Nagas/ Yakshas = earth gods		
Ishta-devatas = personal gods	Kula-devatas = family gods	Graha-devatas = household gods	Grama-devatas = village gods			
			Vira = Guardian god	Mata = Fertility goddess		

and Devatas satisfied mundane, everyday needs, they did not answer more primal issues: Why does the world exist? Do we exist? Who are we? There was a need for God who was greater than the gods. There was need for Ishwara, the supreme lord, Mahadeva, the great god who is God, and Bhagavan, the container of all things.

As a result a divine spectrum now exists within the Hindu pantheon. At one extreme is one rather impersonal God, an abstract spiritual entity, without name or form. At the other extreme are personal gods worshipped by different people, at different times, at different places, for very earthly reasons.

The difference between God and god is that the latter fears death and jealously guards Amrita, the nectar of immortality.

God has no such fear. God never dies, for God was never born. Every time God blinks a god dies. Every time a god blinks a human dies. This idea of relativity between humans, gods and God is captured in the following narrative. It shows that only God can expand and contract time and space.

Revata's Daughter

Revata, ancient king of Dwarka, took his daughter, Revati, to Brahma and asked him to suggest a worthy groom for her. He spent just one day with Brahma, not realizing that one day with Brahma is equal to a thousand years on earth. By the time he returned, his kingdom had disappeared, overrun by forests, and the men on earth had shrunk in size, making him and his daughter giants. Taking pity on Revati, Krishna asked his brother Balarama to swing his plough and touch her shoulder with it. When Balarama followed his brother's advice, Revati shrank in size. Balarama fell in love with her and made her his wife. (Folklore)

For many Hindus, Krishna is God incarnate. He participates in history, walks this earth as a mortal but still retains the power to defy the laws of space and time. Krishna is Ishwara who is Mahadeva who is Bhagavan who is God. God is self-created or svayambhu and self-contained. A god is obliged to participate in the wheel of life; God, on the other hand, has the choice to step in and out. God may submit to the law of Brahmanda but does not depend on it for his existence.

Narada's Doubt

Narada had heard that Krishna had married 16,108 women. 'How can he keep everyone happy?' he wondered. Curious, he decided to visit Krishna's island-city Dwarka. There he found 16,108 palaces. In each palace he found a Krishna with a queen. There were 16,108 Krishnas for 16,108 queens. Krishna had defied the laws of space and time and multiplied himself to satisfy everyone. Narada realized that Krishna was no ordinary human. He was God himself. (Bhagavata Purana)

Krishna is Vishnu and Vishnu is one of the three primary manifestations of God. The other two are Brahma and Shiva. The three manifestations are interdependent. Brahma creates; Vishnu sustains; Shiva destroys. Creation cannot happen without destruction. Or destruction without creation. Sustenance involves both creation and destruction.

Brahma is visualized as a priest, Vishnu as a king and Shiva as an ascetic. Of the three, Brahma is not worshipped. The reasons for

Table The Hindu Trinity

Brahma	Vishnu	Shiva
Creates	Sustains	Destroys
Priest	King	Ascetic
Chases the Goddess	Loves, marries and protects the Goddess	Withdraws from the Goddess
Associated with Saraswati, Goddess as knowledge	Associated with Lakshmi, Goddess as wealth	Associated with Shakti, Goddess as power

this are twofold: one metaphysical and the other historical. From the metaphysical point of view, Brahma represents jiva-atma, the soul seeking answers, hence unworthy of worship. Vishnu and Shiva represent param-atma, the soul that has found the answer. Having found the answer, Vishnu continues to participate in the world while Shiva withdraws from all things worldly. Vishnu's eyes are therefore always open while Shiva's eyes are always shut. Historically, Brahma represents the earlier Age of Rituals when Hindu society gave more importance to the mechanical execution of yagna. In the Age of Worship, yagna faded into the background and with it Brahma. More attention was given to Shiva and Vishnu. Shiva represents the hermit's way of life; Vishnu represents the householder's way of life. In the worship of Shiva and Vishnu, Hindu society was able to resolve its own conflict: to celebrate worldly life or renounce its fettering enchantments.

Hari-Hara

A composite form of Shiva and Vishnu. Shiva, the ash-smeared ascetic, represents the realized soul who withdraws from the world. Vishnu, the gold-bedecked king, represents the realized soul who participates in the world.

There is great rivalry between the worshippers of Shiva, known as Shaivas, and the worshippers of Vishnu, known as Vaishnavas. Each side tries to position one over the other. For devotees, their patron deity is always the svayambhu, self-created, self-contained and self-reliant, and hence greater than the rest. Thus Vishnu is svayambhu for Vaishnavas and Shiva svayambhu for Shaivas. For Shiva worshippers, a human dies when Indra blinks, Indra dies when Brahma blinks, Brahma dies when Vishnu blinks and Vishnu dies when Shiva blinks. Vishnu worshippers disagree with this. They believe Brahma dies when Shiva blinks and Shiva dies when Vishnu blinks. The strategic intent of either narrative is obvious. In the following story, Vishnu is projected as a greater form of God. As Shiva is not worldly, he lacks the dexterity to even protect himself.

Bhasmasura

Pleased with the intense piety of an Asura, Shiva offered him a boon. The Asura asked that any creature he touched should be instantly reduced to ashes. No sooner did Shiva give this power than the Asura decided to try his power on Shiva himself. Fearing for his life, Shiva ran. The Asura pursued him. A desperate and frightened Shiva begged Vishnu to help him. Vishnu took the form of Mohini, the enchantress, and presented his female form to the Asura. Enchanted by Mohini's ravishing form, the Asura stopped chasing Shiva. 'Marry me,' he told Mohini. 'Only if you can dance just the way I do,' said Mohini. The Asura agreed. He observed Mohini's dance carefully and began imitating her movements. He moved his hands, feet, waist, neck and face just as she did. At one point, Mohini touched her

head. The Asura did the same and was instantly reduced
to ashes. Shiva sang songs praising Vishnu, who had rescued
him from certain death. (Vishnu Purana)

In the following story, Shiva is the greater god. Shiva is so
detached from things worldly that the extent of his power has
no boundaries. Like the pillar of fire, he has neither beginning
nor end, no top or base.

Pillar of Fire

Brahma and Vishnu were once embroiled in an argument
as to who was greater than whom. 'I am the father of all
conscious beings, including you,' said Brahma to Vishnu.
'You were born in a lotus that emerged from my navel.
This makes me your creator,' said Vishnu to Brahma. In the
course of the argument, a pillar of fire appeared between
Brahma and Vishnu. Brahma took the form of a goose and
flew upwards to find its top. Vishnu took the form of a
boar and dug into the earth to find its base. Neither was
successful. From the pillar emerged Shiva. Both Brahma and
Vishnu realized Shiva, embodiment of the pillar of fire, was
Mahadeva, greater than any Deva. He was even greater than
both of them because his origin and end were not known.

The difference between the world-affirming Vishnu and the worldly
renouncing Shiva is expressed in their representation. Vishnu
bedecks himself with ornaments and silks and sandal paste and

flowers. Shiva smears himself with ash, wraps himself in animal skins, mats his hair and lets a serpent slither round his neck. Vishnu is associated with domestic fertile cows, Shiva with the virile yet untamed bull. Vishnu is associated with the ocean of milk; as Rama he sits on a throne; as Krishna he is associated with gardens and battlefields. Shiva is associated with snow-capped mountains, caves and cremation grounds. Vishnu is surrounded by all things auspicious and desirable, such as symbols of power, pleasure and prosperity. Shiva is surrounded by all things inauspicious and undesirable, such as ghosts and dogs. Vishnu clearly is a member of society, distinguishing between the appropriate and the inappropriate. Shiva is the eternal outsider refusing to discriminate between gods and demons. For Vishnu, devotees offer bright, fragrant flowers, such as champaka, and processed milk products, such as butter and sweets. Shiva is content with water, raw, unboiled milk and the flowers of poisonous plants, such as dhatura.

Ayyappa

Ayyappa is also known as Hari-Hara-Suta, the son of Vishnu and Shiva. This deity is an attempt at reconciling the devotees of Shiva and Vishnu. He was born after Shiva embraced Vishnu's female form, Mohini. He was raised by a king of Kerala who called him Manikantha. He grew up to be a great warrior who could tame tigers and lions. Like Vishnu, he fought demons and made the earth a safer place. Like Shiva, he renounced his claim to the throne and lived a celibate existence atop a hill.

A male form is essentially incomplete and presupposes the existence of a female form. God cannot be incomplete; hence Brahma, Vishnu and Shiva have female counterparts. There is Saraswati for Brahma, Lakshmi for Vishnu and Shakti for Shiva. Together these three couples embody the Hindu understanding of the ultimate divine.

The Hindu Trinity of God and Goddess

Brahma creates, Vishnu sustains, Shiva destroys, while Saraswati, Lakshmi and Shakti embody knowledge, wealth and power respectively. The male forms of the divine are associated with verbs—creating, sustaining and destroying—while the female forms of the divine are associated with nouns: knowledge, wealth, power. Gods do; Goddesses are. Gods are active; Goddesses passive. Goddesses may be knowledge, wealth and power but it is Gods who are knowledgeable, wealthy and powerful. Thus the male form of divinity represents the subject—he who is sensitive to life and he who responds to life. The female form of divinity represents the object—she who is life.

Uma Maheshwar

The Goddess marries Shiva, the hermit, and makes him a householder. She forces him to open his eyes and see the mirror in her hand. Not by shutting his eyes, but by opening them can God see himself. The Goddess is the object, the mirror, the world. God is the subject, the reflection, the self. Without her, he cannot know himself. Without him, she has no purpose. Both validate each other's existence.

Sometimes devotees identify the creative, sustaining and destructive aspects of God in one entity. Narayana of Vaishnavas or Shiva of Shaivas is the the supreme manifestation of God. The three Goddesses are seen as one, Adi-Maya-Shakti, or simply Devi, the supreme manifestation of Goddess. God is spirit; Goddess is matter. God is soul; Goddess is substance. God is the observer; Goddess is the observation. God establishes artificial values; Goddess is natural phenomena. God is the divine within all beings; Goddess is the divine around all beings. One cannot exist without the other. Without either, there is neither.

Four Heads of the Creator

Here we explore what propels the evolution and shaping of the universe.

The Veda is the earliest compilation of Hindu hymns. It is at least 4000 years old. It wonders how creation began.

Origins

In the beginning,
There was neither Being nor Non-Being
Neither sky, earth, nor what is beyond and beneath.
What existed? For whom?
Was there water?
Death, immortality?
Night, day?
Whatever there was, there must have been one
The primal one (God?)
Self-created, self-sustained, by his own heat,
Unaware of himself
Until there was desire to know himself.
That desire is the first seed of the mind, say seers
Binding Non-Being with Being.
What was above and what was below?
Seed or soil?
Who knows?
Who really knows?
Even the gods came later.
Perhaps only the primal being knows.
Perhaps not.
(Rig Samhita)

The Veda is believed to be of non-human origin, a container of timeless wisdom. Brahma sang these hymns out when he first saw Saraswati. These were transmitted to humans through seers known as Rishis. The seers who sat around Brahma heard four collections of Vedic mantras emerging from his four heads. These collections or samhitas came to be known as Rig, Sama, Yajur and Atharva. Of these Rig Samhita is believed to be the purest transmission.

In the earliest phase of Hinduism, Vedic hymns were chanted mechanically during rituals known as yagna to invoke divine power and change the workings of the world. Kings were the patrons of these grand ceremonies. Then a revolution took place. Sages such as Yagnavalkya and kings such as Janaka challenged the mechanical chanting of mantras. They focused on the ideas being communicated through the hymns. As a result, a thousand years after the Veda was compiled, the Upanishad came into being. This body of scripture is known as Vedanta, the pinnacle of Vedic wisdom. It states that creation involved the splitting of the primal being who is identified as Pursuha.

The Split

In the beginning was the self, the Purusha
Alone, afraid, wondering what made him lonely and fearful
If there was loneliness and fear
There could also be company and pleasure
Restless, he split himself. (Brihad-Aranyaka Upanishad)

The split portion of the Purusha is identified as Prakriti. The two complement each other. In common parlance, Purusha is translated to mean 'man' while Prakriti means 'nature'. Thus Purusha can also mean 'culture' while Prakriti can also mean 'woman'. These translations suggest that in the Hindu world man is equal to culture and woman to nature. Such an interpretation reinforces the popular belief that the Hindu world is patriarchal, with men deciding how the world should be.

There is an element of truth here. But the Veda and the Upanishad were not concerned with gender politics or social issues. While these did influence their thoughts, the primary motivation for these scriptures was metaphysics. Biological symbols were tools to explain complex ideas as to how the world came into being and why.

In the above narrative, the split is not of an androgynous being into man and woman. It is the split between the subject and the object. The subject is the conscious being—that which feels. The object is the stimulating environment—that which is felt. The subject is Purusha. The object is Prakriti. Purusha is the soul; Prakriti is mind and matter. Purusha is the inner reality, without gender, name or form. Prakriti is the outer reality of gender, names and forms. Purusha is still and unchanging, unaffected by

Table Two Halves of Reality

Purusha	Prakriti
Spirit	Matter
Subject	Object
Conscious being	Stimulating environment
Observer	Observation
Inner reality	Outer reality

time or space; it is that which makes the body alive. Prakriti is restless and ever-changing, a product of history and geography; it is the encasement of the soul. Purusha is perfect, hence not of this world, to be defined by negation, neti-neti, not this, not that. Prakriti is everything in this world, hence never perfect, to be defined by affirmation, iti-iti, this too, that too.

That Purusha and Prakriti exist after the androgynous being splits itself informs us that neither does Purusha create Prakriti nor does Prakriti create Purusha. They come into existence simultaneously. Neither is autonomous. Neither can exist independent of the other. Purusha needs Prakriti and Prakriti needs Purusha.

To explain the rather complex metaphysical concept of Pursuha and Prakriti and their complementary relationship, Rishis looked for symbols in nature, in animals, plants and minerals. Examples can never possess all the qualities of the idea, but they help take the attention of the mind in the direction of the thought.

Rishis realized that just as Purusha could not be explained without comparing and contrasting it with Prakriti, the northern direction could not be explained without referring to the southern direction, the right side could not be explained without the left side and man could not be explained without woman. Following this realization, the north, the right side and all things masculine came to represent Purusha while the south, the left side and all things feminine came to represent Prakriti.

Left was chosen for Prakriti because it was associated with the beating heart while the silent right was reserved for Purusha. North with its still Pole Star was most appropriate to represent the soul. South, its opposite, represented matter. Apparently

Table Tantrik Symbols of Vedic Concepts

Type of Symbol	Purusha	Prakriti
Biology	Male	Female
Minerals	Ash	Water
Man-made object	Staff	Pot
Direction	Right	Left
Direction	North	South
Colour	White	Red
Plant	Banyan tree	Banana plant
Animal	Turtle	Serpent
Geology	Mountain	River
Triangle	Upward-pointing	Downward-pointing
Geometry	Dot	Circle
Sound	Om	Shri

unchanging elements of nature such as the banyan tree, the turtle and mountains became symbols of the soul, while rapidly changing elements of nature such as the banana plant, the slithering, moulting serpent and the flowing river became symbols of matter.

The choice of male biology for the conscious being and female biology for the impersonal environment has its roots in Tantra. Unlike the Vedanta, which was the creation of erudite priest–philosophers, the Tantra was the creation of the common man. Both had roots in the Veda, but while one concerned itself with transcendental issues, such as the soul, the other focused on matters more earthy and immediate, such as biology, astrology, alchemy, architecture and fertility. Both had a profound influence on each other. Using biological observations to explain abstract metaphysical notions is a case in point.

In the Tantrik understanding of human physiology, all living organisms possess seed that helps them procreate. Plants, animals and women shed their seed involuntarily during pollination, heat and menstruation. The human male, however, has the freedom to shed his white seed, the sperm, at will or not at all. This made the human male the perfect symbol of a being capable of choice. The human female became the symbol of impersonal nature fettered to the tide of time. Likewise white, the colour of semen, became the colour of the soul within while red, the colour of menstrual fluid, became the colour of matter without.

Lajjagauri

Despite being found in almost every part of India and in every period in history, no scripture identifies this image. Art historians call her Lajjagauri, the shy goddess, more out of convenience because while a covered face suggests modesty, the exposed genitalia certainly does not. The female body suggests the image represents nature. The absence of her face suggests impersonality. Her stance is that of a woman ready to offer herself to her beloved, an act that will give pleasure to the beloved and make her a mother. This image therefore could represent Prakriti: nature—impersonal, pleasure-giving and fertile.

A thousand years after the Upanishad, another revolution took place. People became increasingly theistic. Like the mechanical rites of earlier times, the speculations of the Upanishad did not satisfy the emotional needs of society. There was need for a divinity that was not merely an abstract force invoked during yagna or an abstract idea to be analysed by metaphysicians. There was need for a concrete divinity that could be embodied and personified so that it responded to the human condition in human terms. To answer these needs, epics such as the Ramayana and the Mahabharata and chronicles known as the Puranas came into being. These told the stories of gods and demons, Gods and Goddesses. In them, Purusha was personified as Brahma, Vishnu and Shiva while Prakriti was personified as Saraswati, Lakshmi and Shakti. Stories of Gods and Goddesses were in effect narrative expressions of the interactions between spiritual demands and material needs, between the conscious being and the enveloping environment, between the divine within and the divine without, between Purusha and Prakriti.

In the epics and the Puranas, Brahma is God who creates the world. There are many versions of how this happens, suggesting no one is sure how things began because 'even the gods came later'. What follows is the predominant version.

Birth of Brahma

In the beginning, on the ocean of milk, within the coils of the serpent of time, Narayana stirred out of his dreamless slumber. From his navel rose a lotus in which sat Brahma. Brahma opened his eyes and realized he was alone. Brahma trembled. He wondered who he was. From that desire to know himself, Brahma decided to understand what he was not. First he created four boys, the Sanat-Kumars, out of his thoughts and asked them to produce children. They did not know how. They did not understand why. They disappeared. Then came ten grown men, again out of Brahma's thoughts. These men were the Prajapatis. They knew how to produce children; they asked their father to give them a wife. Brahma split himself into two. From his left half came a creature unlike Brahma or his sons. It was a woman. She was extraordinarily beautiful. Brahma and the Prajapatis were stirred by her beauty. The woman walked around Brahma to pay her respects, for Brahma was her father. Brahma, overwhelmed by desire, sprouted three extra heads, two on the sides and one behind, so that he could look upon her at all times. Discomfited by her father's stare, the daughter rose to the sky. Brahma popped a fifth head atop the other four. This one looked away from Narayana towards the daughter. The daughter ran. Brahma ran after her. As she ran, the daughter took a number of forms, all female: goose, mare, cow, doe. Afraid of losing her, determined to possess her, Brahma kept taking the complementary male forms: gander, horse, bull, buck. Thus different types of jivas came into being. (Brahmanda Purana)

Narayana's slumber represents a state when the consciousness is totally unresponsive to the world around. So deep is the slumber that Narayana is not even aware of himself. This is pralaya, dissolution, the period before the split between Purusha and Prakriti. There is neither observer nor observation. Things have no form or name. Space collapses. Life entropies into a formless, nameless mass—the ocean of milk. Time is no longer sequential. The past, present and future telescope into each other. The serpent of time coils rather than slithers.

Narayana

Narayana is the name of Vishnu as he sleeps a dreamless slumber. When he wakes up, a lotus emerges from his navel in which resides Brahma. This makes him creator of the creator. However, the lotus is connected to Vishnu's navel just like a mother's placenta, suggesting that the interactions of Brahma with the world, that is the Goddess, nourishes him. There is thus a symbiotic relationship between creator and creation, God and Goddess. Hence the line from the Rig Samhita, 'He created her and she created him. They are born of each other.'

Narayana is the purest conceivable form of Purusha. He is consciousness that is uncrumpled, uncreased, unknotted, unpolluted. The waking up of Narayana, the blooming of the lotus, the birth of Brahma and his sons are various stages in the crumpling of this consciousness. Curiosity about the self is the impulse of this crumpling process. The crumpling gives rise to Brahma, the intellect, that is able to distinguish the self from all that the self is not—mind and matter. Brahma's desire for children is the desire of consciousness to have a fruitful interaction with the world, the ultimate goal being knowledge of the self.

The first four sons of Brahma are called the ancient ones, Sanat-Kumars, because they come into being before the creation of the sense organs. Without the sense organs, the mind does not know the material world. The mind unruffled by sensory stimuli is pure, hence the mind-born sons of Brahma are described as innocent, pre-pubescent boys. Such a mind has no desire to act. It is incapable of producing children or answering Brahma's questions.

Brahma realizes that for a fruitful interaction with the world, he needs channels that receive stimuli and transmit actions. This results in the birth of the ten sons, the Prajapatis, five representing the five sense organs (eyes, ears, nose, tongue, skin) and the other

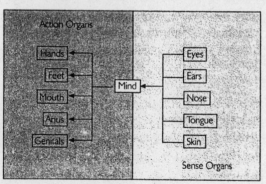

The Ten Sons of Brahma

five representing the five action organs (hands, feet, mouth, anus, genitals). Following the birth of the Prajapatis, Brahma becomes aware of the world around him, that is the Goddess. This awareness takes the form of a sexual stirring. Unlike the first four sons of Brahma, the Prajapatis are mature, capable of responding to erotic stimuli.

The Goddess exists even during pralaya. But no one observes her as all senses are dormant. This unobserved Goddess is known as Yoga-nidra, she who exists during God's dreamless slumber. When Narayana wakes up, the lotus blooms and Brahma opens his eyes. The senses come alive. Yoga-nidra becomes Yoga-maya, stimulating the senses.

Yoga-maya is called Brahma's daughter because she owes her origin to him. If Brahma had no questions, if Brahma felt complete, if Brahma had been self-contained, he would never have 'looked' for answers: the observer would have had no observation, and the world would never have been 'created'. Another name for Yoga-maya is Usha, meaning 'dawn' because her arrival is like the dawn, the hour of awakening. She is also called Shatarupa, meaning she of infinite forms. Like the world she represents, the Goddess is mercurial, constantly transforming. She goes around and envelopes Brahma as soon as she appears.

Sensations and actions fill the mind with memories, desires and ideas. These are the three extra heads of Brahma. A point comes when the consciousness is so crumpled by external inputs that a fifth head appears, atop the previous four, looking away from Narayana. This is the ego—that part of the mind that constantly seeks validation and approval from the world around.

Table Elements of Creation

Metaphysical Concepts	Mythological Characters	Gender
The soul	Narayana (the sleeping Vishnu)	Male
Mind's capacity to discern and distinguish things (the intellect)	Brahma	Male
Mind's constituents before the appearance of the source of stimuli: absence of memories, absence of desires, absence of knowledge and absence of ego	4 Sanat-Kumars	Male
Mind's constituents after the appearance of the source of stimuli: presence of memories, presence of desires, presence of knowledge and presence of ego	4 extra heads of Brahma	Male
Mind's inward and outward channels: 5 sense organs and 5 response organs	10 Prajapatis	Male
Ego	Fifth head of Brahma	Male
Material world, the source of stimuli and destination of responses, the external matrix	Usha	Female

The narrative emphasizes that the ego has no independent existence; it is a reaction to worldly stimuli. The ego takes Brahma away from knowing his true self: Narayana.

Spurred by the ego, Brahma seeks to possess the Goddess, control her. She takes many forms, as is her nature, and slips away like water from a clenched palm. To keep up with her, Brahma changes his forms. When she becomes a goose, he becomes a gander. When she becomes a cow, he becomes a bull. In effect, Brahma loses his own identity and acquires an identity that depends on the outside world. As the chase proceeds, Brahma forgets the reason he created the world in the first place. The objective of self-realization gives way to the quest for self-preservation, self-propagation and self-actualization.

The word chitta is used for the moulding consciousness; it connects the mind to the soul, manas to atma, Prakriti to Purusha. Narayana is param-atma, the uncrumpled consciousness of God. Interactions with the world, the Goddess, crumple chitta and introduce memories, desires, ideas and ultimately the ego. This crumpling process is represented by the sprouting of Brahma's heads. The five-headed Brahma is jiva-atma, the crumpled consciousness of the unenlightened, ignorant, ego-dominated jiva. The four-headed Brahma who sings the Veda is the crumpled consciousness of the enlightened, wise, soul-dominated jiva.

A jiva can be defined as any living creature who fears death, hence is constantly involved in acts of self-preservation and self-propagation. A jiva contains a jiva-atma, is sensitive to the environment and constantly engages with it in its quest to survive and find meaning in life. While the original uncrumpled state, param-atma, is the same for all jivas, the differences in crumpling

Table Param-atma and Jiva-atma

Param-atma	Jiva-atma
Unknotted chitta	Knotted chitta
Uncrumpled consciousness	Crumpled consciousness
Soul of God	Soul of a jiva
Unaffected by memories, desires, ideas or ego	Conditioned by memories, desires, ideas and ego
Witness to a world that is limitless	Witness to a world that is limited
The destination of yoga or sensory discipline	The result of bhoga or sensory indulgence

are responsible for the different **personalities** of different jivas. Crumpling can increase or decrease, depending on how the jiva responds to stimuli. In principle, every jiva can potentially uncrumple its chitta so that the jiva-atma becomes param-atma. This ability creates a craving for the original uncrumpled state. It makes the jiva restless for that perfection, that primal peace, the dreamless slumber.

Brahma is the grandfather of all jivas. His sons marry the many forms of Shatarupa. Together they give birth to different types of jivas. Through the seed of Brahma's sons flows jiva-atma into the jiva. From the wombs of their wives come the different types of flesh. In the following narrative, serpents and eagles have a common

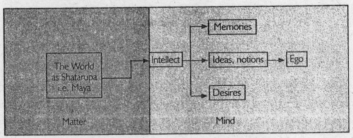

The Five Heads of the Deluded Brahma

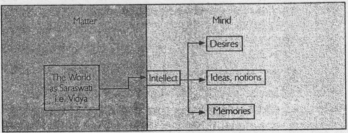

The Four Heads of the Enlightened Brahma

father, Kashyapa. Hence all possess a crumpled chitta. Because they have different mothers, serpents slither on the ground while eagles fly in the air. The difference is superficial, that of the flesh. This difference allows each one to interact differently with nature.

Grandchildren of Brahma

From Brahma's thoughts came seven seers, the Sapta Rishis. One of the seven seers had a son called Kashyapa. Kashyapa had many wives. On Aditi, Kashaypa fathered the Devas, on Diti he fathered the Asuras, on Vinata he fathered Garuda, the eagle, and on Kadru he fathered the Nagas, serpents. Kashyapa was also the father of Manu, from whom came humans, the Manavas. Like Kashyapa, Vaishrava was another of Brahma's grandsons. He fathered the race of Rakshasas and Yakshas, malevolent and benevolent forest spirits. (Narada Purana)

All jivas are distributed across three worlds: the earth, the celestial regions and the subterranean realms, all located below the abode of Brahma, Satya-loka, the realm of truth.

- Devas live in Amravati, a city located above the sky in the celestial realm known as Swarga, where they are entertained by dancing damsels known as Apsaras and musicians known as Gandharvas.
- Asuras and Nagas, commonly described as demons and serpents, live in Hiranyapura and Bhogavati, cities located under the earth in the realm known as Pa-tala.

- Manavas live on earth, Bhu-loka, along with plants, animals and wild forest spirits such as Yakshas and Rakshasas. When Manavas die they go to the land of the forefathers, Pitr-loka, and stay there until it is time to be reborn.

The three worlds are indicative of the three worlds every living creature resides in simultaneously. There are three objective worlds of all individuals: the private world, the social world and the natural world. Then, there are the three subjective worlds: the apparent world perceived by the senses, the imaginary world of dreams and the unconscious world of desires, memories and conditioning. Subjective or objective, every world provokes the jiva to act.

Table Three Worlds

Mythological	Swarga-loka, Bhu-loka, Pa-tala
Subjective	Perceived, Imagined, Subconscious
Objective	Private, Social, Natural

Significantly, Brahma never creates the three worlds. He merely populates it with jiva. God may observe and organize the world, but at no point does he ever create the world physically. Even the Upanishad presupposes the existence of Prakriti when it says Prakriti comes into being after Purusha splits itself from it. Essentially, the two are one. Two sides of the same one. Purusha never creates Prakriti. Both exist together and forever. Creation is awareness of the difference. Likewise, a jiva never creates its world: it is simply made aware of it. The purpose of life then is not to change what one did not create. Rather it is to explore this world, experience it, understand it and by doing so discover the truth about oneself.

Of all jivas, the chitta is most crumpled in the Asuras and least in the Devas. To indicate this the Devas are said to reside in a realm that is closest to Brahma's abode while the Asuras reside farthest. In terms of degree of crumpling of the chitta, Rakshasas and Manavas are not as bad as the Asuras and not as good as the Devas. The abode of Rakshasas and Manavas is therefore neither below the earth nor above the sky. It stands in between. On earth. This is reinforced in the following story.

The Doorkeepers of Vishnu

The four Sanat-Kumars wanted to pay their respects to God who resides in Vaikuntha in the form of Vishnu. When they arrived at Vaikuntha, the doorkeepers Jaya and Vijaya did not let them enter as Vishnu was sleeping. The sages decided to wait. Some time later they approached the gates once again. Again the doorkeepers did not let them enter. 'Because the lord is still asleep,' they said. This happened the third time too. Piqued, the sages cursed the doorkeepers, 'Because you stopped us from meeting God three times, may you be born three times. May you experience death three times. May you know what it is to be away from the presence of God for three lifetimes.' When Vishnu woke up and learned what had transpired, he apologized to the sages. He then promised to do everything he could to help his doorkeepers return to Vaikuntha because they had only been doing their duty. The two doorkeepers were born as two Asura brothers, Hiranayaksha and Hiranakashipu. Hiranayaksha dragged the earth under the sea, forcing Vishnu to take the form of a boar, plunge into the waters, gore him to death and raise the earth back to the surface. Hiranakashipu tortured his own son, Prahalada, a devotee of Vishnu, for chanting the name of God, forcing Vishnu to manifest as the man-lion Narasimha and tear him to shreds. Hiranayaksha and Hiranakashipu were then reborn as Ravana and Kumbhakarna, two Rakshasa brothers who believed might is right and threatened all codes of civilized conduct. Their actions forced Vishnu to take the form of Rama and destroy them. Then Ravana and Kumbhakarna were reborn as Shishupala and Dantavakra, two villainous humans who valued personal ambition over social order. Their behaviour forced Vishnu to descend as Krishna and kill them. Death at the hands of God released Jaya and Vijaya from the Asura, Rakshasa and Manava forms and ensured their return to Vaikuntha, where they resumed their roles as doorkeepers. (Bhagavata Purana)

Jaya and Vijaya are Devas. As doorkeepers of Vishnu, they are closest to God. But a curse transforms them into Asuras and takes them far away from God. The flesh is impermanent. Hence both the Deva and the Asura forms of Jaya and Vijaya are impermanent, lasting only for a lifetime. The form taken in subsequent lives depends on events of the previous life. After living their life as Asuras, they become Rakshasas and live above the earth, indicating their chitta is not as knotted as it was before. In the life that follows, they become Manavas, humans, with greater unknotting. Finally, the original state of chitta is restored. Jaya and Vijaya become Devas and return to the doorsteps of Vaikuntha.

While God descends on earth to interact with 'demonic' Asuras, Rakshasas and Manavas, he does not let the 'pure' Sanat-Kumars meet him. This is because the purity of the Sanat-Kumars is not the result of wisdom: it is the product of ignorance. They have never engaged with the world. They have never known the flood of sensations or struggled with the tyranny of memories, desires, ideas and ego. They have never known the Goddess, either as mother, wife or daughter. They may be pure enough to reach the gates of Vaikuntha, but not worthy enough to see the sleeping Vishnu who is param-atma. To see God, they must act, respond to worldly provocations, suffer moral and ethical dilemmas and make appropriate choices. Provocation finally comes in the form of Jaya and Vijaya, who do not let them enter Vaikuntha. Response takes the form of a curse. Instantly a series of events happen. Narayana wakes up and rushes to the door. This story reinforces the idea that unless one lives life and interacts with the world the idea of God has no meaning. Without knowledge of the Goddess, there can be no realization of God.

After living out their curse, Jaya and Vijaya return to Vaikuntha as doorkeepers. But they stand outside the door, not inside, suggesting there is still some uncrumpling left to be ironed out before they reach God. The images of Jaya and Vijaya look very similar to Vishnu's. They hold in their four hands the conch-shell trumpet, the discus, the lotus and the mace. But they are not Vishnu. Hence they possess fangs, a reminder of their demonic deeds and the remnant crumpling in their souls. The Devas may be closest to God but they are not God. Like demons and humans, their chitta is plagued with restlessness. They too seek the serenity of the param-atma.

Da

The Devas, who live above the sky and the stars in the celestial city of Amravati, were not happy. The Asuras, who live under the earth in the golden city of Hiranyapura, were not happy. Nor were the Manavas, humans, who live on earth, below the sky and the stars. So all three went to their grandfather, Brahma. Looking at their unhappy faces, Brahma said, 'Da.' What did that mean? No one knew. The Devas deciphered it to mean 'Damyata', which means moderation. Their craving for the pleasures of life had to be kept in check if they sought happiness. The Asuras deciphered it to mean 'Daya', which means compassion. Their desire to dominate the three worlds had to be kept in check if they sought happiness. The Manavas deciphered it to mean 'Datta', which means generosity. Their urge to hoard wealth had to be kept in check if they sought happiness. (Katha Upanishad)

The concept of different types of jivas inhabiting different types of worlds is an attempt to represent the plural nature of existence. No two creatures are the same. No two plants, no two animals, no two men or two women are the same. Every creature experiences the world differently. Every jiva is unique. But in essence everyone is the same: a Brahma sitting on the lotus that rises from the navel of Vishnu, looking for answers in three worlds. Hence the Vedic maxim 'Aham Brahmasmi'.

Yama's Book of Accounts

In this section the governing principles of the universe—desire and destiny—are analysed.

In the Upanishad, a young boy called Nachiketa asks Yama, the god of death, what happens after death. Yama at first hesitates to answer the question. For even the gods are not sure. He then gives an answer which forms the foundation of Hindu understanding of life and death.

Yama states that the body has two parts: soul and flesh, atma and sharira. The atma is immortal. Only the sharira can die. The soul is surrounded by three shariras:

1. Sthula-sharira or the flesh
2. Sukshma-sharira or the mind
3. Karana-sharira or the causal body, memory of deeds

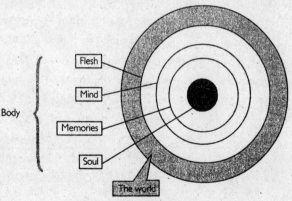

The Three Bodies

Death happens when Yama's messengers, known as Yama-dutas, drag the mind out of the flesh. When this happens, the

flesh becomes insensitive and unresponsive to all worldly stimuli. It starts to decay. The flesh needs to be cremated and the skull cracked open so that the soul and the causal body can escape. During funeral ceremonies that follow, the survivors encourage the soul wrapped in the causal body to travel across Vaitarni to the land of the dead, where Yama rules and the Pitr reside.

Pitr are the ancestors, the dead awaiting rebirth, subjects of Yama. They have no flesh, hence no gender. They have no mind, hence no ego. But they have a soul and a causal body. In this form they stand before Yama. He determines their fate. Before pronouncing his judgement, Yama always consults Chitragupta, his accountant, who meticulously maintains a record of a jiva's actions in its lifetime. The causal body is essentially Chitragupta's accounts book, a record of past deeds.

Being an accountant, Chitragupta classifies these deeds as debt or equity. Selfish actions that make demands of the world and indulge the ego are debt-incurring actions. Selfless actions where the ego sacrifices its pleasure for the sake of the world are equity-earning actions. If there are debts that a Pitr has to repay, Yama ties him with a noose and fetters him to the world, forcing him to be reborn. If there are no debts to repay, Yama lets the Pitr go, liberated from the obligation of rebirth. Thus rebirth and release are the two possible destinations for the dead.

Hindu funeral rites involve the use of both fire and water. The body is cremated and the bones and ashes cast into the river. Fire represents the fire of moksha or release. The river represents samsara, the realm of rebirths. The two possible destinations of the soul are thus symbolically acknowledged. Yama, who determines the journey the soul will take, is therefore not merely god of death but also god of destiny.

Yama

Yama is the dark and impersonal ruler of the dead. He rides a buffalo and moves slowly towards all creatures from the day they are born. Yama is slow but relentless in his pursuit. He carries a noose with which he binds all creatures to samsara until they repay their karmic debts and enjoy their karmic equities. He also carries a mace, indicating that he is Dharma, god of order, totally dispassionate in his judgements. He determines the future circumstances in the life of a jiva, based on the record of past deeds.

According to the law of karma, every jiva is obliged to experience the reactions of all actions. Yama is the keeper of this law. When it is clear that a Pitr has debts to repay and must take birth in samsara once again, Yama determines the circumstances of its next life: time of birth, time of death, type of body, type of family and finally its fortunes and misfortunes. All these are based on Chitragupta's records. Life is thus a manifestation of the karmic balance sheets. Yama carries out his duty dispassionately. No emotions move him. There is no bias in his decision. He is therefore Dharma, god of order. In the following story, Yama is a victim of the very laws he upholds.

Vidura's Past Life

A group of thieves was caught hiding in the hermitage of a sage called Mandavya. The sage, who was deep in meditation, was not even aware of their presence. But the soldiers who caught the thieves refused to believe him. Accusing him of assisting the thieves, they impaled him. Mandavya asked Yama why he had suffered such a fate. Yama replied it was the result of cruel acts performed when he was a child—he had caught flies and passed the rib of a coconut leaf through them for his amusement. Mandavya felt that actions of children are done in innocence and should not be part of Yama's accounts book. Enraged, he cursed Yama that he would take birth on earth in the womb of a low-caste woman. His father would be a king and his mother would be the king's mistress. Although he would have all the qualities of a king, he would never be allowed to wear the crown on account of his low birth. Because of this curse, Yama took birth as Vidura, the uncle of the Kauravas and the Pandavas, who despite his worthy qualities could never be king. (Mahabharata)

Vidura's misfortune can be traced to a curse. Likewise a fortune can be traced to a boon. Curses and boons are narrative tools to explain the concept of karma. A curse is a manifestation of debt. A boon is a manifestation of equity. Curses and boons link action to reaction. Yama's judgement is the action; Mandavya's curse is the reaction. Reactions in turn become stimuli that provoke a response. Mandavya's curse is the stimulus; Yama's acceptance of that curse without resistance is the response.

If debt and curses bring sorrow, equity and boons bring happiness. In the following story, Dhruv's suffering at being denied his father's affection is offset when he wins the affection of God. God's affection comes through a boon.

Dhruv

Uttanapad had two wives, Suniti and Suruchi, each of whom had borne him a son. Suruchi was his favourite. One day, Suruchi found Suniti's son, Dhruv, sitting on Uttanapad's lap. She pulled him down and drove him away saying, 'Only my son can sit on his lap.' Dhruv went to his mother, who consoled him saying, 'You can always sit on the lap of Vishnu who is God, everyone's father.' Dhruv, a child of five, ran out of his house and went to the forest in search of Vishnu. 'Where can I find him?' he asked the sages. 'He is everywhere. Just pray to him and he will come.' Dhruv began to pray. After his prayers, he opened his eyes and there was no Vishnu. 'You need to pray very hard if you want God to come to you,' said the sages, amused and touched by the child's innocence. Dhruv then took a decision to sit in one place, shut his eyes and pray until Vishnu appeared before him. Minutes turned to hours. Hours turned to days. Days turned to weeks. Weeks to months. Dhruv did not move or open his eyes or stop his prayers. The sages watched in disbelief. Birds and animals watched over him in amazement. The spirits of the forests gathered around him in awe. Finally, Vishnu had no choice but to appear before the lad. 'What do you want?' he asked. Dhruv opened his eyes, all excited, and replied, 'To sit on your lap.' Vishnu picked up Dhruv and placed him on his lap. No one can move Dhruv from God's lap. He sits there still, as the Pole Star in the skies. (Folktale based on Bhagavata Purana)

It is difficult to establish where the effects of a boon end and the influence of a curse begins. The following story demonstrates how in the long run a boon can be a bad thing while a curse can be a good thing.

Rama's Exile

Dasharatha's favourite wife, Kaikeyi, had saved his life in battle. In gratitude he gave her three boons. On the eve of her stepson Rama's coronation she asked for the three boons: 'Let Rama renounce the throne, let him live in the forest as a hermit for fourteen years and let my son, Bharata, rule in his place.' Dasharatha had no choice but to fulfil her wishes. As Rama left the city, Dasharatha remembered an unfortunate event that had occurred in his youth. During a hunting trip he had accidentally shot a young man called Shravana, the only child and caretaker of a blind couple. As they mourned the death of their son, the couple cursed Dasharatha that he would die of a broken heart following separation from his son. During his exile in the forest, Rama killed Ravana, much to the delight of the Devas, who were oppressed by this king of the Rakshasas. (Ramayana)

Had Dasharatha not been cursed, had Kaikeyi not misused her boons, Rama would never have gone into the forest and Ravana would never have been killed. The effects of curses and boons telescope into each other, weaving the plots of a narrative.

An overview of Hindu narratives shows an obsession with curses and boons. They are used to explain situations. They take the narrative forward. Curses and boons are essentially narrative tools to explain the idea of karma. Nothing in the Hindu world happens spontaneously. Every event is a reaction to the past, the result of a curse or a boon. Fortune is predestined. Misfortune fated.

But destiny is not inflexible. It can change. In the following story, a princess overpowers her destiny with the help of a boon given to her by Yama himself.

Table Actions and Their Reactions in the Mahabharata

Action	Reaction
Ambalika becomes pale when Vyasa makes love to her	Ambalika's child, Pandu, father of the Pandavas, is born an albino
Ambika shuts her eyes when Vyasa makes love to her	Ambika's child, Dhritarashtra, uncle of the Pandavas, is born blind
Gandhari accidentally crushes 100 turtle eggs when she is a child	Gandhari witnesses the death of her 100 sons, the Kauravas, at the hands of the Pandavas
Kunti serves Durvasa dutifully	Durvasa gives Kunti a boon which will serve her well in the future; using it she can call upon any Deva and have a child by him
Pandu accidentally kills a sage and his wife while they are making love	Pandu is cursed that death will strike if he ever makes love to his wives, Kunti and Madri
A princess constantly craves the embrace of her sage husband	She is reborn as Draupadi, who is given five husbands
Arjuna refuses to make love to Urvashi on the grounds that she was married to his ancestor Pururava	Urvashi curses Arjuna that he will lose his manhood
Arjuna is proud of his archery, Bhima of his gluttony, Nakula of his beauty, Sahadeva of his wisdom	These four Pandavas are denied entry into Indra's paradise

Savitri

Savitri, a princess, was the only child of her father. She fell in love with Satyavan, a prince whose father had been driven out of his kingdom by his enemies, and so lived in abject poverty in the forest. Her father opposed this marriage not only because Satyavan was poor but also because Satyavan was destined to die within a year of marriage. Savitri followed her heart nevertheless. At the appointed hour, Yama hurled his noose and took Satyavan's life out of his body. Savitri followed him. 'Go back and cremate his body,' he advised her. She refused to do so and kept following him into the land of the dead. Exasperated, he offered her three boons so that she would go away, 'Anything except the life of your husband.' Savitri first asked that her father get a son and heir. Then she asked that her father-in-law regain his kingship. And finally she asked that she be the mother of Satyavan's sons. 'So be it,' said Yama and continued on his journey to the land of the dead. After some time he noticed that Savitri was still following him. 'You gave me your word that you would return to the land of the living,' he said. 'You give me no choice. You said I would be the mother of Satyavan's children. How can a dead body make me a mother? I must therefore follow Satyavan's jiva-atma into the land of the dead.' Yama realized he had been outwitted. As custodian of the laws of karma, his boons had to be realized. The only way for Savitri to bear Satyavan's children was to make Satyavan alive again. And that was done. (Mahabharata)

Savitri's determination earns her a boon just as Dhruv's determination earns him a boon. This determination has its roots in desire, the intense craving for something. Desire is a powerful force in Brahmanda, as powerful as destiny.

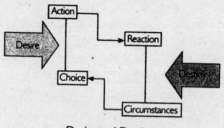

Desire and Destiny

According to the Veda, before all things came desire. It is desire that caused the restlessness which led to creation. Without desire, God would not have opened his eyes to observe the Goddess. In the Puranas, desire takes the form of a god called Kama. Kama is an archer whose arrows struck Brahma, awakening his senses, making him aware of his daughter and her myriad forms.

Kama

Kama is a dark and handsome archer with mischievous eyes. He rides a parrot. With five flowers as arrows, he rouses the five senses. A sugar cane, rich with the sap of life, serves as the shaft of his bow while bees, seeking the nectar of worldly delight, serve as the bowstring. The red colour of the parrot's beak represents possibilities while the green colour of its feathers represent fruition. It is desire that links possibilities to fruition. For without desire there is no action; without action there is no reaction. Without action and reaction nothing can exist.

Yama swings his noose and fetters the jiva to his destiny. Kama shoots his arrow and injects desire in the jiva. Destiny manifests as worldly stimuli while desire influences choice of response. Destiny is determined by past deeds. Desire influences future actions.

Table Kama and Yama

Kama	Yama
Passionate	Dispassionate
Pleasure seeker	Account keeper
Flies on a parrot, swiftly in any direction	Travels on a buffalo, slowly in one direction
Holds a bow	Holds a noose
Shoots an arrow away from him and forgets about the damage caused to the jiva	Drags the jiva towards him and forces jiva to repay debt
Irresponsible	Extremely responsible
God of desire	God of destiny

In the following story, Bharata's desire fetters him to the wheel of rebirths. He escapes only when he desires moksha so much that he is able to endure his destiny without resistance.

Bharata Is Reborn

Bharata was the son of Rishabha. Like his father, he was a great king. After completing his duties as king, he handed over the crown to his son and became an ascetic and went to the forest, where he meditated and sought self-realization on the banks of a river. One day he saw a pregnant doe quenching her thirst not far from where he sat. Suddenly they both heard the roar of a hungry lion. The pregnant doe gave birth at that moment. The faun dropped into the river. Without bothering to save it, the doe, terrified of the lion, ran away. Bharata saw the newborn faun floating in the river. Filled with compassion, he rescued it and raised it as his own child. When he died, the last thought in Bharata's mind was the well-being of the faun. In his next life, Bharata was born a deer but he remembered his previous life, how he had been distracted from the goal of self-realization by worldly matters. He decided to take residence in the hermitage of sages, hear their words of wisdom and begin once more his quest for liberation from the wheel of rebirths. In the life that followed, Bharata regained human form. He was born into the family of a priest. After his father died, his half-brothers treated him like a servant. He was asked to watch over the cows. One night he was captured by devotees of Kali, who planned to sacrifice him to the goddess. But no sooner was he brought before the image of Kali than he glowed. This aura was the result of his wisdom, his understanding of life. The Goddess appeared, drove her devotees away and blessed Bharata to continue his journey of self-realization. Bharata was then made captive by the servants of a king who were one person short of palanquin bearers. Bharata carried the palanquin but could not stay in step with the other palanquin bearers. The king kicked him on the head. Bharata kept quiet. The king questioned who he was. Bharata's answers made the king realize that his palanquin bearer was a highly evolved soul, one who had understood the true meaning of life and no longer needed to be part of things worldly. He fell at Bharata's feet and sought blessings. After this life, Bharata was reborn no more. (Bhagavata Purana)

Bound with destiny, propelled by desire, the jiva faces a moment of choice: to accept destiny, fight it or avoid it. Choice of response, and the obligation of facing its consequences, rests solely with the jiva, as Ratnakara discovers in the following story.

Ratnakara

Ratnakara was a highway robber and killer. One day he attacked the sage Narada. 'Why are you doing this?' asked the sage. 'For my family,' replied Ratnakara. 'Will they pay the price of your misdeeds?' asked Narada. 'Yes, they will. After all, I am doing this for them,' said Ratnakara confidently. Narada requested Ratnakara to check with his wife and son if this was really true. Ratnakara ran home and asked his wife and son if they would share the burden of his karmic debts. 'No,' said his wife. 'Why should I? My duty is to keep your household. Your duty is to provide for it. How you choose to provide for your family is your concern, not mine.' Ratnakara realized that ultimately a jiva is responsible for his actions. He gave up his life as a criminal and became the author of the great epic Ramayana that chronicles the life of a prince whose lets his destiny, not his desires, shape his life. (Ramayana)

There are different types of action depending on the motivation behind them. The motivation may be self-preservation, self-propagation, self-actualization or self-realization. Each action may incur debt or generate equity. A response to a stimulus may repay an old debt, incur a new debt, spend existing equity or generate additional equity.

Table Types of Actions

Action	Reaction
Indulging the ego	Incurs debt
Greed, ambition, domination	Incurs debt
Suffering misfortune silently	Clears debt
Detached fulfilment of duties	Clears debt
Paying fees, i.e. dakshina	Clears debt
Thanksgiving gifts	Clears debt
Pilgrimage, i.e. tirtha yatra	Clears debt
Devotion, i.e. bhakti	Clears debt
Worship, i.e. puja	Earns equity
Sacrifice, i.e. bali, yagna	Earns equity
Charity, i.e. daan	Earns equity
Enjoying life	Spends equity

Sometimes debt can be incurred quite accidentally, without even wanting to.

Nrga, the Lizard

King Nrga of the Ikshavaku clan decided to distribute cows to all the priests in his kingdom in charity. As the distribution was in progress, one of the cows gifted to one priest ran away, re-entered the royal enclosure and was gifted to another priest. Later both priests came to the king, claiming the cow as their own. Nrga realized what had happened and apologized. He offered both priests new cows to settle the matter. But the priests refused. They left the king's court furious. Because of this one incident, Nrga was reborn as a lizard. (Bhagvata Purana)

In the following narrative, a hunter earns equity and attains moksha quite by chance.

The Offering of Bel Leaves

A hunter got lost in the forest and took refuge on top of a tree to protect himself from wild animals during the night. The tree happened to be the bel tree, which is much loved by Shiva. The branches of the tree shook as the hunter climbed to the top, causing leaves to fall on a rock below. This rock was Shiva's sacred symbol, the linga. Thus the hunter inadvertently made offerings to Shiva, pleasing the God, who then granted the hunter freedom from the cycle of rebirths. (Linga Purana)

This story demonstrates the power of God who is greater than the gods, including Yama. God can override the decisions of Yama, grant release even to those who deserve to be trapped in the cycle of rebirths.

Ajamila

Ajamila was not a good man. He never did his duties as father, brother, husband or son. He was a gambler, drunkard and lazy lout. On his deathbed he called out to his son, 'Narayana, Narayana.' The son did not come to him and he breathed his last. Narayana is the sacred name of Vishnu who is God. Consequently, Vishnu's servants prevented Yama's servants from taking Ajamila's soul and causal body to the land of the dead. Ajamila was taken to Vaikuntha to stay eternally in the presence of God. (Bhagavata Purana)

Instead of being taken to the realm of Yama across the Vaitarni, Ajamila ends up in Vaikuntha, the abode of Vishnu. In the following story, intense devotion to Shiva helps Markandeya reach Kailasa, the abode of Shiva.

Rescue of Markandeya

Markandeya was doomed to die at the age of sixteen. On the eve of his sixteenth birthday, Markandeya decided to worship Shiva. At the appointed hour Yama appeared. Markandeya, however, had not finished his prayers. He requested that Yama wait for a while. Yama laughed, reminding the boy that death waits for no one. He flung his noose and began dragging out Markandeya's life breath. Markandeya cried out to Shiva. In response to his cries, Shiva appeared, kicked Yama away and took his devotee to his celestial abode, where he lived, forever sixteen, free from the fear of death. (Shiva Purana)

Gajendra Moksha

Vishnu striking a crocodile with his discus to liberate the king of elephants trapped in its jaws. The king of elephants represents the jiva. The lotus pond represents the pleasures of life. The crocodile is the price of that pleasure. God liberates the jiva from the obligation to pay that price. Devotion to God makes it possible for any creature to enjoy samsara without incurring debt.

Vaikuntha and Kailasa represent the Hindu heaven, the destination of released souls. These are located above the three worlds and must be distinguished from Swarga, the Hindu paradise, abode of the Devas. Swarga is very much a part of samsara, governed by the rules of karma, fettered by time and space. In Vishnu's heaven and Shiva's heaven these rules and fetters do not apply.

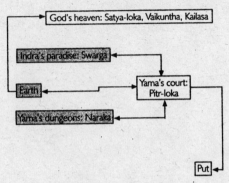

Three Worlds and More

The following story demonstrates how a mortal king comes to sit among the gods by suffering his fate without resistance. It also distinguishes repaying debt from earning equity through the concepts of dakshina and daan. Dakshina is a fee paid for services. It clears debt. Daan is an act of charity. It earns equity.

Harishchandra

Harishchandra, king of Ayodhya, was a good king, much loved by his people. One day, while out hunting, Harishchandra accidentally disturbed a sage's ascetic practices aimed at acquiring occult powers. 'How can I make up for your loss?' asked the king. 'I am a sage. I want nothing of the material world. You have, however, taken away everything I desire from the spiritual world.' A guilty Harishchandra said, 'To make up for your loss, I offer you all that I possess in the material world.' Harishchandra gave the sage his crown and his kingdom and retired to the forest with nothing but the company of his wife, Taramati, and his son, Rohita. As he was leaving, the sage stopped him, 'You must give me a fee for accepting the kingdom to clarify that what has been given is not an act of charity. It is a ritual offering to relieve you of the burden of guilt. A thousand gold coins will suffice.' To pay the fee, the penniless Harishchandra sold himself, his wife and his son in the slave market and gave the earnings to the sage. Harishchandra was purchased by a chandala, keeper of a crematorium. Taramati and Rohita were purchased by a priest, who kept them as servants. Once king and queen, Harishchandra and Taramati accepted their fate without protest. One day Rohita was bitten by a venomous snake and he died instantly. When Taramati brought the corpse to the crematorium, Harishchandra mourned for his son but refused to cremate him until his wife paid the fee his master charged for burning a body. Taramati had no money. 'Then give me the clothes you wear. Otherwise our child will not be cremated.' Taramati obeyed. As she began disrobing, the gods appeared in the crematorium, amazed by this display of absolute submission to fate. They decreed that Harishchandra was fit to reside in Swarga. (Bhagavata Purana)

Swarga is the abode of the Devas, the destination of jivas who have only equity and no debts in their karmic accounts books. Swarga is a place of opulence and abundance. Every material wish is fulfilled there without effort. Since all needs are satisfied, its residents are forever in a state of delight.

Actions that take a jiva towards Swarga are known as punya, merit-generating actions. Actions that take a jiva away from Swarga are known as paap, demerit-generating actions. Paap incurs debt. Punya earns equity. Harishchandra reaches heaven because of punya. In the following story, Nahusha enters Swarga because of punya but is thrown out because of paap. Thus stay in Swarga is not permanent.

Table Constituents of Swarga

Constituent	Description
Kalpataru	A tree that never withers and bears any fruit one wishes for
Kamadhenu	A cow that provides all one wants
Chintamani	A jewel that fulfils every wish
Akshaya-patra	A pot that is always full of grain and gold
Amrita	Nectar that keeps the Devas healthy and ever-youthful
Varuni	Wine that brings dreams of joy without the fear of hangover
Apsaras	Damsels well versed in the 64 ways of pleasing the 5 senses

Nahusha

Indra had killed the son of his teacher. He had to leave Swarga to atone for this crime. So the Devas decided to appoint Nahusha as their ruler until Indra returned. Nahusha was a Manava, a king who had attained great merit by performing numerous yagnas. Nahusha was pleased to be king of Amravati. He enjoyed the fruits of the Kalpataru, the milk of Kamadhenu and the dance of the Apsaras. He rode on Indra's elephant, Airavata, and even hurled Indra's thunderbolt. But he wanted more—access to Indra's queen, Sachi. Sachi was horrified by Nahusha's impertinence. To teach him a lesson she requested him to come to her on a palanquin carried by seven Rishis. Nahusha ordered the Rishis to carry the palanquin and the Rishis obeyed. One of the Rishis was Agastya. He was short and could not walk as fast as the others. Nahusha, impatient to reach Sachi, kicked Agastya on the head. Furious, Agastya cursed that Nahusha would leave heaven and return to earth, not as a human but as a serpent. (Mahabharata)

Just as a jiva enters Swarga by accumulating equity, a jiva sinks to Naraka under the burden of debts. Naraka is everything Swarga is not. It is a place of great suffering, struggle and stress.

Death of the Pandavas

Thirty-six years after ruling Hastinapur, the five Pandava brothers and their common wife, Draupadi, decided to renounce the world. They believed that since they had established a righteous kingdom on earth they had earned enough equity to enter Swarga effortlessly with their mortal bodies. To reach the abode of the Devas, they decided to climb the Meru. Unfortunately, on the way, they slipped and died one by one. The first to die was Draupadi, imperfect because she preferred Arjuna over her other husbands. Then it was Sahadeva, imperfect because he was smug about his knowledge, followed by Nakula, imperfect because he was arrogant about his good looks. Then fell Arjuna, imperfect because he was always jealous of other archers, and then Bhima, imperfect because he was a glutton. Only the eldest Pandava, Yudhishtira, reached the realm of the Devas, located high above the skies. There he found to his horror all the Kauravas and no sign of his brothers. 'Why?' he asked. Yama explained, 'Because the Kauravas died as warriors are supposed to, on the battlefield. This earned them so much merit that it wiped out all their debt.' Yudhishtira demanded to know where his brothers and his wife were. He was taken below the earth to a dark and terrible place full of misery and torture. It was Naraka. Yama explained, 'They are experiencing the reactions of their actions.' Yudhishtira refused to leave Naraka as he could not abandon his brothers and his wife in their hour of pain. Yama smiled and said, 'This is temporary. Once the debt has been repaid, they will join the Kauravas in Swarga. You too have had to experience Naraka for the one and only white lie you spoke in your lifetime.' (Mahabharata)

That the unrighteous Kauravas reach Swarga while the righteous Pandavas reach Naraka indicates that the laws of karma are not easy to fathom. Merits and demerits are earned in complex ways, not all known to man.

In the following story, Krishna who is God is cursed by Gandhari, mother of the Kauravas. In being responsible for the death of the unrighteous Kauravas, Krishna may be a hero for many, but for the mother of those he killed he is villain. Paap and punya are thus many a time matters of opinion.

The Curse of Gandhari

With the help of Krishna, the Pandavas killed their cousins
the Kauravas and established righteousness in the land.
Gandhari, the mother of the Kauravas, was inconsolable
in her grief. She cursed Krishna that he would witness the
death of his children and kinsmen, after which he would
suffer an ignominious death at the hands of a common
hunter. (Mahabharata)

The story of the Kauravas in Swarga informs us that there is
always hope in the Hindu world, even for the worst of villains.
Paap can be overcome by punya; debt can be offset with equity;
desire can override destiny; a resident in Naraka can eventually
end up in Swarga. But there is one place where there is no hope.
That place is called Put. It is reserved for Pitr who are trapped
in the land of the dead with no hope of being reborn.

Rebirth can only happen when an offspring or descendant
left behind in the land of the living produces a child. Those
who die childless have no one in the land of the living who can
ensure their rebirth. They are doomed to stay in Put. That is
why a son and a daughter are known as put-ra and put-ri in
Sanskrit, meaning 'deliverers from Put'. By producing a child,
a living person not only repays his debt to his ancestors he also
helps a Pitr escape from the land of the dead into the land of
the living.

Pitr

Pitr are commonly described as forefathers. But they are simply souls of the ancestors—male or female. As per Hindu mythological vocabulary, male forms are used to represent the spirit and soul while female forms are used to represent matter and flesh. The old men represent atma. The ropes represent the causal body that fetter them to samsara. If all their descendants on earth refuse to produce children, they cannot ever get out of samsara. They are trapped forever until Pralaya, the death of the world.

In the following story, a celibate sage is troubled by visions of his suffering ancestors who are trapped in Put, unable to escape until he fathers a child.

Agastya's Forefathers

Agastya did not want to marry. He performed yoga in the forest, refused to react to sensory stimuli and generated tapa. But he was troubled by visions of old men hanging upside down from a beam, with rats gnawing the ropes, threatening to drop them into a bottomless black hole. The old men identified themselves as Pitr, the ancestors.

'Produce children and help us be reborn. If you don't we are doomed to oblivion with no chance of entering the land of the living, no chance of interacting with samsara, no chance of discovering our true identity, no chance of being released from the cycle of rebirths. You owe your life to us. Now repay the debt by giving us life.' (Mahabharata)

The Hindu obsession with marriage and childbirth can be traced to the concept of Put. In the Mahabharata, the character Devavrata earns the title of Bhisma because in order to make his father happy he takes a bhisma or terrible vow that condemns him to Put for all eternity.

Devavrata Becomes Bhisma

Devavrata was the crown prince of Hastinapur. His father, Shantanu, fell in love with a fisherwoman called Satyavati, who refused to marry him until he promised her that only her sons would be the inheritors of his throne. Shantanu could not give such a promise. Realizing the cause of his father's unhappiness, Devavrata voluntarily renounced his crown. 'But what if your children challenge the claims of my children?' asked Satyavati. To put her mind to rest Devavrata declared he would never touch a woman or father a child. (Mahabharata)

When a Hindu man or woman dies, his or her children perform the funeral rites known as shraadh. During the ceremony, three

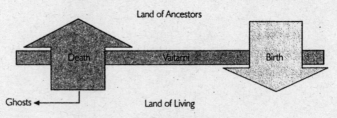

Land of Ancestors

Death

Vaitarni

Birth

Ghosts ←————

Land of Living

Land of the Living, Dead and Undead

generations of ancestors are invited to a meal and by offering of rice cakes there is a symbolic reiteration of the promise to produce children and repay the debt to ancestors.

If shraadh is not performed, the causal body lingers in the land of the living in the form of a ghost or Preta unable to cross the river Vaitarni. When people are murdered by highway robbers, when a person dies in an accident, and no one knows that they are dead, no one performs their shraadh. The causal body of such persons transform into Preta. A ghost haunts the land of the living. In the Hindu world, ghosts are not God-less creatures. They are not exorcized. They are in essence Pitr, somebody's forefathers. The difference is that they are angry and restless because nobody has helped them reach the land of the dead and they are not welcome in the land of the living. A haunting is the cry of a lost soul demanding attention. To rid a place of haunting, the ritual of atma-shanti is required; this is simply a modified shraadh in which those haunted by ghosts promise to do everything in their power to help the rebirth of the Preta.

Rebirth is important. In the womb, the dead are wrapped in flesh and mind so that they once again enter the land of the living and interact with the material world. And without interacting

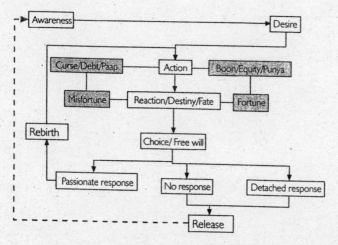

Rebirth and Release

with the material world, the soul can never realize its true nature, hence never get release.

There are no temples dedicated to Brahma. There are no temples dedicated to Kama or Yama either. Perhaps because they spin the wheel of samsara. Perhaps because one prefers worship of solutions rather than of problems. All rituals and prayers are aimed at stemming the restlessness of the soul. Offerings are made to gods and goddesses who change the course of destiny and fulfil desires. When neither is possible, worshippers turn to God, seeking strength to cope with existence. Or they observe the Goddess, seeking an understanding of the puzzle called life.

Trapped between desire and destiny, stimuli and responses, fate and free will, the jiva craves for peace with the three worlds his three bodies engage with. Hence all Hindu rituals end with a triple appeal, 'Shanti, shanti, shanti'. Let me be at peace with myself, my world and the rest there is.

2
The Square of
Vishnu and Lakshmi

In which the cultural codes are distinguished from natural laws

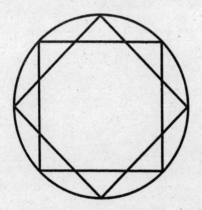

The square, with its sharp edges, is the most artificial of shapes.
When drawn within the circle of the universe, it best represents
culture. Different cultures have different values, hence the square
of culture can be oriented in various ways, but always anchored
to the rim of the circle at its corners. All cultures, however
different, depend on nature for their survival.

Vishnu

Vishnu is visualized as a blue-coloured warrior god, bedecked in gold and silk, adorned with a garland of forest flowers, who holds in his four hands a conch-shell trumpet announcing his presence in the world, a discus representing the rhythm of life, a mace to punish law breakers and a lotus to reward law abiders. Vishnu rests on the coils of a serpent until disorder forces him to ride into battle on his eagle and set things right. Vishnu's serpent represents a stable earth, regularly regenerating itself with the seasons and tides. Vishnu's eagle is the sweeping wind of change—the revolution that brings back hope. Serpent and eagle, they will always be in conflict.

Vishnu is God who organizes the world. Vishnu introduces rhythm into nature so that all the changes of Brahmanda become predictable, hence manageable. With rhythm come waves and troughs. For Vishnu therefore the Goddess has two forms: Lakshmi, the desirable one, and Alakshmi, the undesirable one. Lakshmi is the fertile and auspicious wave of nature—the day, the waxing moon, the high tide, the spring, the rains and the harvests. Alakshmi is the barren, inauspicious trough of nature—the night, the waning moon, the low tide, the hot, dry summers and the bitter-cold winters.

Vishnu also domesticates nature to establish culture. Within culture, man can look beyond survival and explore his potential. He can generate wealth and create art. Society comes with rules and regulations, roles and responsibilities, milestones that give life direction and standards that create hierarchy. At the top of the hierarchy is Lakshmi, all that society admires. Below is Alakshmi, all that society shuns.

Lakshmi

Bejewelled and dressed in red, seated on a lotus, holding a pot overflowing with grain and gold, Lakshmi is the Goddess embodying pleasure, prosperity and power that culture harvests out of nature. She is enchanting and whimsical. Holding on to her is a constant struggle. White elephants, rare and precious, salute her with offerings of water. Beside her sits her twin sister, Alakshmi, goddess of poverty, strife and misfortune, as an owl, demanding acknowledgement.

Never-ending Battles between Devas and Asuras

This section throws light on value judgements that come with culture so that the beneficial aspects of nature—those within the square—are appreciated while the rest outside the square are rejected and condemned.

A recurring theme in Hindu mythology is the battle between the Devas and the Asuras. The Asuras are the incorrigible troublemakers of the Hindu world who need to be constantly defeated by the Devas.

Sunda and Upasunda

Sunda and Upasunda were two Asura brothers who could not be defeated so long as they fought together. They drove the Devas out of their celestial city of Amravati and became lords of the three worlds. Knowing that it would be impossible to defeat them by force, the Devas turned to cunning: they sent the most beautiful Apsara, Tilotamma, to seduce them. No sooner did the brothers lay eyes on this nymph than they wanted to make her their chief queen. Tilotamma said, 'I can belong only to one, the one who is the stronger of the two.' Both brothers were desperate to possess her. Not wanting to give her up, they started fighting with each other. Blows were exchanged but both were equally matched. So they ended up killing each other at Tilotamma's feet. The Devas danced in joy. (Mahabharata)

Both the Asuras and the Devas invoke God in their quest to be triumphant. Typically, the story begins with an Asura invoking God and seeking immortality. God refuses to give such a boon, for all jivas are mortal. So the Asura asks for a boon that makes him almost invincible, hence almost immortal. Using this boon, the Asura launches an attack against the Devas and drives them out of Amravati. The Devas then invoke God, who defeats the Asuras either through force or through trickery. God is thus responsible for the alternating victories and defeats of the Devas and the Asuras.

Hayagriva

A horse-headed Asura called Hayagriva once invoked Brahma and sought from him the boon of immortality. When such a boon was not forthcoming, he sought a boon by which he could be defeated by none other than another being who also had a horse's head, also called Hayagriva. Such a creature did not exist in the three worlds and so no one could defeat Hayagriva. In time, Hayagriva stole the Veda, the book containing all the wisdom in the world. There was pandemonium in the three worlds. The Devas did not know what to do. So they went to Brahma, who advised them to take the help of Vishnu. When the Devas went to Vishnu, they found him taking a nap, resting his chin on his bow. Taking the form of termites, the Devas ate into the bowstring so that the bow shaft snapped with such force that it severed Vishnu's neck. To save the headless Vishnu, the Devas sacrificed a horse and placed its head on his neck. Vishnu thus transformed into a horse-headed being. The Devas named him Hayagriva and begged him to defeat the Asura Hayagriva. Vishnu challenged

Hayagriva to a duel, smote him with his mace and restored
the Veda to the world. Brahma then restored Vishnu's head.
(Skanda Purana)

Varaha

The Asura Hiranayaksha once dragged the earth under the sea. The earth-
goddess's cries for help reached Vishnu, who took the form of a boar called
Varaha, plunged into the sea, gored the Asura to death, placed the earth-
goddess on his snout and raised her to the surface. As they rose, the boar-
god embraced the earth-goddess, causing mountains and valleys to form.
He plunged his resplendent tusks into her body, causing her fertile soil to
sprout plants of every variety.

The form taken by God to defeat the Asuras varies from story
to story. For Vaishnavas it is usually an incarnation of Vishnu,
such as Varaha. For Shaivas, it is either Shiva himself or one of
his sons, Kartikeya or Ayyappa or Ganesha. For Shaktas, the Devas

turn to the Goddess when both Vishnu and Shiva express their inability to defeat the Asura.

Durga Kills Mahisha

Mahisha, the Asura king, obtained from Brahma a boon by virtue of which no plant, animal, man, demon or god could kill him. Thus empowered, Mahisha drove the Devas out of the celestial regions. They went to their creator, Brahma, who directed them to Vishnu, who directed them to Shiva. Shiva directed all the Devas to release their powers and create out of it a single entity containing all their strength. The Devas spat out their energy as flames, which fused into a single blinding blaze out of which emerged a magnificent warrior woman with eight arms, called Durga, who rode into battle on a lion. Mahisha fell in love with her and desired her as a wife. He sent his commanders with the marriage proposal only to hear her declare that she would marry one who defeats her in battle. Mahisha sent many a warrior to bring her, by force. But she killed each one of them. Finally Mahisha attacked her, taking the form of various animals—lion, elephant, buffalo. After a great battle that lasted nine nights she finally impaled him with a trident. She succeeded because Mahisha had not bothered to seek protection from women. (Markandeya Purana)

The peace that follows the defeat of Mahisha, or any Asura for that matter, is only temporary reprieve. Soon a new Asura appears and repeats the cycle of war and victory. War seems almost a reaction to peace and vice versa.

There is something rhythmic in the shifting fortunes of the Devas and the Asuras. Neither is defeated permanently; both are matched equally. This suggests that the existence of Asuras is necessary for the world. Without them there is imbalance.

God never destroys an Asura. The Asura is simply put in his place. In the Hindu world, the Asuras live under the ground in the golden city called Hiranyapura. The Devas live in the celestial city above the sky called Amravati. The space in between is the battleground. In the following story, Bali is generous but his presence above the earth disturbs the balance of the three worlds. Order is restored only after Vishnu shoves him under the earth.

Three Steps of the Dwarf

The Asura king Bali defeated the Devas and became lord
of the three worlds. He was loved by all because of his
generosity. The Devas, impoverished in defeat, approached
Vishnu, who said, 'Bali's generosity will be his undoing.'
Vishnu approached Bali in the form of a dwarf and asked
as an offering three paces of land. Bali agreed without a
moment's hesitation. The dwarf instantly turned into a
giant. With two paces he covered the sky and the earth.
With the third he shoved Bali to the subterranean regions.
(Vamana Purana)

Trivikrama

Vishnu turning into the giant who conquers the three worlds, hence called Trivikrama. The Asura king Bali, shoved under the earth, rises up annually at harvest time. In Kerala, his return is marked by the festival Onam while in North India his return is marked by Diwali, the festival of lights, when Lakshmi enters households. Curiously, all harvest festivals are associated with the death of Asuras. Dassera is associated with the killing of Mahisha by Durga, and Diwali with the killing of Naraka by Krishna and the defeat of Bali by Trivikrama. The association of the death of Asuras with the harvesting of crops is not a coincidence. As keepers of Sanjivani Vidya, Asuras are the restorers of the earth's fertility. Only by killing the Asura and cutting the crop can the earth's bounty be harvested.

The association of Asuras with the subterranean world, with harvest, with Bali's generosity and the fact that their city is made of gold suggest that the Asuras are seen as the keepers of wealth. All wealth—whether plant or animal or mineral—ultimately has its origin under the ground. Even Lakshmi, the goddess of wealth, is said to reside in Pa-tala—the realm below the ground. The Devas release the Asuras' subterranean wealth. Surya, the sun-god, coaxes plants to move towards the sky with his warmth and light. Chandra, the moon-god, causes the tide to rise and fall, helping in the harvest of fish and salt. Indra, the sky-god, hurls his thunderbolt, forcing monsoon clouds to release rain. Vayu, the wind-god, wears down mountains, forcing out rivers. Agni, the fire-god, melts rocks and releases metals. Together they draw Lakshmi out.

Indra

Indra rides a white-coloured elephant and hurls thunderbolts that cause dark rain-bearing clouds to release rain. Indra is thus the ruler of the skies and bringer of rain. His elephant is the white cloud that appears after the monsoons. Following his victory, the red earth becomes green with vegetation. The overflowing rivers, the bountiful harvest and the cool autumn breeze are Indra's trophies of war taken by force from the Asuras. But then Indra indulges in victory, and submits himself to a life of pleasure, losing it all. So the battle has to be fought again, every year, the eternal cycle of renewal and fertility.

But while the Devas can release and redistribute wealth, they cannot regenerate wealth. That power resides with the Asuras, whose priest, Shukra, possesses Sanjivani Vidya, the secret of resurrecting the dead. He can resurrect the Asuras killed by the Devas, restore the earth's fertility stripped by the Devas in harvest time. This makes the Asuras not mere enemies, but complements of the Devas in the cycle of life.

Asuras are said to be strong when the sun is making its southern journey from the house of Cancer to the house of

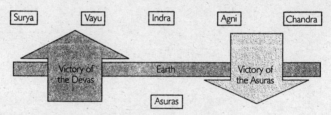

The Churning of Wealth

Table Comparison between the Devas and the Asuras

Devas	Asuras
Kashyapa's children by Aditi	Kashyapa's children by Diti
Brihaspati, lord of Jupiter, is their guru	Shukra, lord of Venus, is their guru
Brihaspati, who has two eyes, hence balanced, represents rational thought	Shukra, who has one eye, hence imbalanced, represents creative intuition
Live in the skies	Live below the ground
Powerful from winter solstice to summer solstice, as days grow longer and warmer	Powerful from summer solstice to winter solstice, as days grow shorter and colder
Pull wealth above the ground	Drag wealth under the ground
Wealth redistributors	Wealth regenerators
Possess Amrita, the elixir of immortality	Possess Sanjivani Vidya, the science of bringing the dead back to life
Enjoy music and dance and tend to be insecure	Tend to be generous and arrogant
Sachi, a form of Lakshmi, is Indra's wife	Pulomi, a form of Lakshmi, is their sister

Capricorn, when days become shorter and nights colder. Asuras are strong when the moon is waning. Asuras are stronger at night. Together with the Devas, the Asuras complete the year, the month and the day.

Lakshmi is sometimes described as Pulomi, the sister of the Asuras, and sometimes as Bhargavi, the daughter of their priest, Shukra. Indra abducts her and installs her as his queen, Sachi. But he invariably loses her when he indulges in the pleasures of women and wine, and has to struggle to win her back. For this he needs the help of the Asuras.

The Curse of Durvasa

The sage Durvasa brought Indra a fragrant garland as a gift. But Indra was too drunk to take notice. He let it hang on the trunk of his elephant, who threw it on the ground and then crushed it under his feet. Angered by this display of irreverence, Durvasa cursed that Indra would lose all his splendour. Lakshmi at once disappeared from Amravati. Gloom descended on the world. All was barren and bereft of joy. The Devas went to Vishnu, who said that since Lakshmi had dissolved herself into the ocean of milk she had to be churned out. This, however, could not be done without the help of the Asuras. The Asuras missed Lakshmi too. So the Devas and the Asuras forgot their differences and came together to churn the ocean. Mount Meru was used as the spindle of the churn. Vishnu took the form of a turtle and prevented the mountain from sinking. Vishnu's serpent, Sesha, wound himself round the mountain. The Devas caught his tail, the Asuras

grabbed his neck, and the churning began. The ocean
frothed and fumed for aeons until finally the waters
coagulated to reveal fabulous treasures, the most delightful
of which was Lakshmi. (Padma Purana)

The Devas and the Asuras serve as the force and counterforce of
the churn, whose spindle is made up of the axis of space and
whose rope is made up of time itself. Vishnu stablizes the churn.

The ocean of milk represents the limitless possibilities of the
world. All matter is in a state of entropy until the Devas and the
Asuras agitate it. What emerges as a result are treasures

Table   Treasures Churned Out of the Ocean of Milk

Representation of	Treasures from the Ocean of Milk	Name
Power	Flying horse	Ucchaishrava
	Conch-shell trumpet	Panchajanya
	Bow	Saranga
	White elephant	Airavata
Pleasure	Nymph	Rambha
	Garland of flowers	Vaijayanti
	Wine	Varuni
	God of love	Kama
	God of health	Dhanavantari
	Nectar of immortality	Amrita
Prosperity	Wish-fulfilling cow	Kamadhenu
	Desire-manifesting tree	Kalpavriksha-Parijata
	Dream-realizing gem	Chintamani-Kaustubha
	Pot of plenty	Akshaya-patra
	Goddess of prosperity	Lakshmi
Pollution	Cosmic poison	Halahala

representing power, pleasure and prosperity, all things that make worldly life worth living.

Along with symbols of power, pleasure and prosperity comes pollution in the form of a viscid mass called Halahala. In some narratives, this is the venomous vomit of the serpent that is used to churn the ocean. Pollution is an inevitable component of any manufacturing process. Halahala is a by-product of all the good things that are churned from the ocean. No one wants this terrible substance. So the Devas turn to the hermit Shiva. Since he is indifferent to worldly things, he does not distinguish between things that are desirable and things that are undesirable. In his eyes, Halahala is no different from Amrita, the nectar of immortality. He consumes the poison. In Vaishnava literature, Halahala is embodied in Alakshmi, the goddess of misfortune, the twin sister of Lakshmi. Just as nothing wonderful can be produced without the simultaneous production of waste, Lakshmi is always accompanied by Alakshmi. Those who ignore the twin sister of the goddess of fortune do so at their peril. Alakshmi is the goddess of strife. Unless she is acknowledged, fortune always brings with it calamity.

Lakshmi and Alakshmi

The twin sisters, Lakshmi and Alakshmi, approached a merchant and asked him who of the two was more beautiful. The merchant knew the consequences of angering either one. So he said, Lakshmi is beautiful when she enters a house and Alakshmi when she leaves it.

Consequently fortune entered the merchant's house and misfortune left it. (Folklore)

Lakshmi is associated with sweets, and Alakshmi with sour and pungent things. Sweets are therefore kept inside the house while sour lemons and pungent chillies are hung outside the house at the doorway. Lakshmi enters the house to eat sweets while Alakshmi eats lemons and chillies at the doorway and turns away satisfied. Both are acknowledged and respected but only one is welcomed.

The Devas and the Asuras divide the treasures of the ocean of milk among themselves. But the most prized treasure is Amrita, the nectar of immortality. That the Devas and the Asuras crave for it is a reminder that both are jivas, hence mortal. Vishnu ensures that only the Devas consume Amrita.

Mohini Tricks the Asuras

Both the Devas and the Asuras wanted to drink Amrita. They fought over it. Suddenly there appeared in their midst Mohini, the female form of Vishnu. She was so ravishing that both the Devas and the Asuras fell in love with her. She offered to distribute the Amrita among the Devas and the Asuras. Everyone agreed and the fighting stopped. Mohini looked at the Asuras with seductive eyes and distracted them while she poured the nectar down the throat of the Devas. Before the Asuras realized what was happening, the Devas had become immortal. They drove the Asuras to their subterranean realm and claimed the treasures of the ocean of milk for themselves. (Vishnu Purana)

Unlike Brahma, who treats the Asuras and the Devas equally, Vishnu clearly sides with the Devas. This favouritism ensures that the wealth that emerges from the ocean of milk stays above the earth, enriching human society. Vishnu is thus a worldly form of God, patron of culture, the lord of Lakshmi.

In the battle between the Devas and the Asuras, the victory of the Devas is profitable to humans. This makes them 'gods' worthy of hymns and offerings. There are no hymns or offerings in yagna for the Asuras. They hoard wealth under the ground, hence are deemed 'demons'.

Rama's Kingdom and Sita's Chastity

This section explores the construction of society through the domestication of nature and the disciplining of the mind.

While the Devas pull wealth out of the earth and the Asuras pull it back in, another battle rages on earth—the battle between Manavas and Rakshasas. The battle between the Devas and the Asuras is a vertical one, a struggle between the realms above and below the earth. The battle between Manavas and Rakshasas, on the other hand, is a horizontal one, between culture and nature.

Rakshasas, like Asuras, are often identified as demons. But a more appropriate word for them would be barbarians, jivas who follow the law of the jungle, known in Hindu scriptures as matsya nyaya or the code of fishes. According to this code might is right, big fish eat small fish. This code offers no reprieve for the weak, the helpless, the downtrodden. Only the fit may survive.

While the code of matsya nyaya is suitable for animals, it is not suitable for humans as humans have the faculty of reason—they can discipline natural urges of sex and violence and tame the instinct to dominate the weak. Manavas, the descendants of Manu, are expected to follow the code of dharma. This code is based on roles and responsibilities. Every creature is bound by duty. This duty bridles desire. It helps in creating a space where even the weakest can thrive.

In the realm of Manavas, sex is acceptable within marriage for the sake of procreation; violence is acceptable only in defence of the pursuit of food. Rakshasas do not respect the laws of marriage. Violence, for them, is a tool to dominate the world. In the following story, Rama and Sita represent the code of dharma while Ravana and Surpanaka represent the law of the jungle.

The Abduction of Sita

Ravana was the king of the Rakshasas and Surpanaka was his sister. Surpanka once saw a handsome hermit in the forest. He was Rama, prince of Ayodhya. Palace intrigues had forced Rama to live in the forest as a hermit for fourteen years. His brother Lakshmana and his wife, Sita, had followed him to the forest to share his suffering. Surpanaka approached Rama and asked him to make love to her. He refused on the grounds that he was married. 'Go to my brother. He has no wife here,' said Rama. But Lakshmana too turned her down because he had a wife back in Ayodhya.

A frustrated Surpanaka attacked Sita, intent on killing her so that with Sita out of the way Rama would reconsider his decision and be her lover. Sita screamed for help. Immediately the two brothers came to her rescue. Lakshmana caught hold of the Rakshasa woman and cut her nose, her ears and the tips of her breasts to teach her a lesson that she would never forget. Surpanaka howled in pain and ran to her brother, who swore vengeance. To punish the two brothers, Ravana decided to abduct Sita, the cause of his sister's unhappiness. He sent a golden deer that so enchanted Sita that she begged Rama to capture it. When Rama did not return for a long time, a restless and nervous Sita begged Lakshmana to look for him. Before leaving, Lakshmana traced a line around Rama's hut. 'Stay within at all times,' he advised his sister-in-law before setting out to look for Rama. While the brothers were away, Ravana came near Rama's hut disguised as a sage and begged Sita for food. Sita invited him in. Ravana refused to enter. He claimed that he was prevented by rules of propriety for she was another man's wife, all alone in the house. Sita then stretched out her hand from within the hut to feed Ravana. Ravana took offence to this. This was no way for a hostess to behave, he said. Bound by the dharma of hospitality, Sita stepped out to feed her guest. Ravana immediately shed his disguise and carried Sita away to Lanka, his golden city on the island of Trikuta. (Ramayana)

Lakshmana-rekha, the line that Lakshmana traces around Rama's hut, is the divide between nature and culture. Within the line

Rama's law applies. Outside is the wilderness, the realm of Ravana. Within there is regard for the law of marriage; without there isn't any. Within, Sita is Rama's wife. Outside, she is a woman for the taking. Ravana knows that if he enters Rama's hut and forces himself on Sita he will be judged by the rules of society. But when he forces himself on Sita outside the Lakshmana-rekha, he will be judged by the laws of the jungle. Within, he will be the villain who disregarded the laws of marriage. Outside, he will be hero, the great trickster.

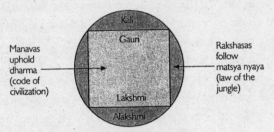

Manavas uphold dharma (code of civilization) → Kali / Gauri / Lakshmi / Alakshmi ← Rakshasas follow matsya nyaya (law of the jungle)

The Fence of Lakshmana

On his way to Lanka to rescue Sita, Rama befriends a race of beings called Vanaras. Vanaras are described as monkeys because they behave like animals. Their king, Vali, behaves like a typical alpha male: he drives all his rivals out of the foraging grounds and refuses to share any female with them. Rama finds himself surrounded by the bachelor monkeys, exiled from the monkey land of Kishikinda, led by Vali's brother, Sugriva. Sugriva seeks Rama's help because his wife has been forced to be part of the royal harem. Rama promises to help. Not as an arbitrator between the brothers but as a strategist who plans the fall of Vali. For in the world of monkeys, there is no concept of justice. Force is the only vocabulary.

Death of Vali

Sugriva challenged Vali to a duel. While they were busy fighting, Rama, who was hiding in the bushes, drew his bow to shoot an arrow and kill Vali. Unfortunately, both brothers looked very much alike and Rama did not know whom to kill. Unable to overpower his brother, Sugriva ran for his life. He then challenged his brother a second time, this time wearing a garland of forest flowers to distinguish himself. The plan worked. Rama was able to shoot an arrow straight through Vali's heart. With Vali dead, Sugriva became king of Kishkinda. He made Vali's wife his queen and accepted Vali's son, Angada, as his heir. In gratitude, he ordered his monkeys to help Rama rescue Sita. (Ramayana)

Rama behaves like Ravana here. He distracts Vali with Sugriva's challenge just as Ravana distracted him with the golden deer. He kills Vali through an act of trickery that is acceptable in the jungle but not in civilized society. In other words, Rama uses the law of the jungle against the very people who follow it. Vali accuses Rama of being a cheat but Rama refuses to feel guilty: those who live by the law of the jungle must be ready to die by the law of the jungle.

But with the coronation of Sugriva, there is a change in the mindset of the monkeys. Typically, after his victory, Sugriva would have killed the children of the previous leader and forgotten all the help he had received. Instead he adopts Vali's son, Angada, and makes him his heir. He then raises an army of monkeys that helps Rama build a bridge to Trikuta, launch an attack on Lanka, defeat the Rakshasas, kill Ravana and rescue Sita.

Rama thus converts the monkeys from followers of matsya nyaya to followers of dharma. Sugriva displays the two characteristics that distinguish a person of dharma: he protects the weak and always keeps his word.

At no point is vengeance the aim of the war against the Rakshasas. Rama seeks to restore order. Rama is the champion of culture.

Rama

Rama, embodiment of cultural perfection, kills the ten-headed Rakshasa king Ravana, who personifies the law of the jungle. Rama's bow is the symbol of poise and balance. Rama always obeyed his parents; Ravana did not. Rama gave up his kingdom for his brother; Ravana usurped Lanka from his brother Kubera, the king of Yakshas. Rama was always faithful to his wife, Sita, while Ravana had many wives in his harem and he raped many more women. Rama ruled for his people; Ravana ruled for himself. Rama represents the perfect man and his kingdom, Rama Rajya, represents the perfect society. Ramayana, the epic dealing with his life, is therefore read in Hindu households.

Culture can exist only when nature is domesticated. This is often a violent act. The forest needs to be fenced and burned down to create the field. Society will decide what seed will be sown, what is crop and what is weed, what is good and what is bad. The following story describes how the Pandavas establish their great city by destroying a great forest, home to many birds and beasts. Without this sacrifice the city cannot be created.

Burning of Khandavaprastha

The Pandavas had inherited the wilderness of Khandavaprastha, where they planned to build a city. The fire-god, Agni, promised to help them if they allowed him to feed on the flora and fauna of the forest. The Pandavas agreed, and Agni's flames soon engulfed the forest. All the residents—birds, beasts, demons and serpents—were burned in the conflagration. The Pandavas shot all those who tried to escape. They even created a canopy of arrows over the forest so that the rain-god, Indra, who had been summoned by the beasts, could not put out Agni's flames. In the land that was cleared the Pandavas built the fabulous city of Indraprastha. (Mahabharata)

Nature constantly threatens to overwhelm culture. Defending culture from this threat is a never-ending struggle. The Harivamsa and several Puranas tell the story of Krishna's early life in a

settlement of cowherds, Gokul, located in Vrindavana, a forest
of tulsi shrubs. It is an idyllic life with cows grazing in the pastures,
cowherds playing the flute and milkmaids churning butter. But
danger is never far away. Various malevolent spirits keep
disrupting the harmony of the village. The adventures of Krishna
are all about how he succeeds in keeping them at bay. But security
is never permanent. Another threat lurks round the corner.
Krishna has to be on guard always.

Life in Gokul and Vrindavana

Putana, a wet-nurse with poison for milk, placed Krishna
on her breasts, intent on killing him. Krishna did not
suck out the milk. Instead he sucked out her life. A
demon hid himself in the wheels of a cart and tried to
run Krishna over when he was barely able to crawl.
Krishna kicked the cartwheel and smashed it to
smithereens. Another demon took the form of a
whirlwind and tried to sweep Krishna away. Krishna
caught the demon by the scruff of his neck and choked
him to death. Demons took the form of horses, bulls,
pythons and donkeys and threatened the well-being of
Krishna's cows and friends. Krishna killed them all with
a smile on his face. The venom of Kaliya, the king of
Nagas, poisoned the waters of the river Yamuna. Krishna
caught Kaliya by his tail and danced on his hood, forcing
Kaliya to submit and leave the river. Indra, king of the
gods, tried to wash away Krishna's village with a
thunderstorm. Krishna raised a mountain and turned it

into a gigantic parasol under which all the cows, cowherds and milkmaids of his village took shelter. A forest fire threatened the grazing cows until Krishna opened his mouth and swallowed Agni, the fire-god. (Harivamsa)

Krishna atop Kaliya

Nagas or serpents slip under the earth and slither on top. This close association with the earth makes them the perfect representatives of the earth's fertility, to be worshipped for a bountiful harvest and for children. Just as the earth renews its fertility each year, the Naga sheds its old skin and replaces it with a new one at regular intervals. The image of Krishna dancing on Kaliya's hood indicates Krishna's domestication of the earth's fertility for the benefit of his devotees.

Culture needs to thrive but not at the cost of nature. Dharma must not only domesticate nature, it also needs to ensure there is harmony between nature and culture. The following narrative describes the end of one society and the rise of another. The earlier king, Vena, is unable to maintain the delicate balance. His son, Prithu, strives hard to do so.

Prithu and the Earth-Cow

King Vena did not respect dharma. Angry, the earth-goddess refused to bear fruit. When the sages realized what was happening they picked up blades of grass that turned into weapons and killed Vena. The sages then churned his dead body. The polluting elements were cast away. This substance turned into a nasty-looking creature that was driven into the forest. The creature was the forefather of the Nishadhas, or forest tribes. From the pure remnants the sages created the perfect king, Prithu, who was given the bow of sovereignty by the gods. Prithu asked the earth to release her wealth. She refused and ran away in the form of a cow. Prithu chased her, raised his bow, subdued her by threatening to shoot her and finally reassured her that he would uphold dharma. He then led all the living beings to milk her by the code of dharma, under his watchful eye. (Bhagavata Purana)

In the Rig Samhita, culture is described, as is Purusha, with a head, arms, trunk and legs. Thus culture is a creation of the conscious being, the jiva. An imposition over Prakriti. Society is an artificial construct, not a natural phenomena. It involves the domestication of nature by man, for man. It also involves the domestication of man.

Balarama

Krishna's elder brother Balarama is said to be an incarnation of a serpent. He was was once so tired that he did not have the strength to go to the river to take a bath. He ordered the river-goddess Yamuna to come to him. The goddess refused. Enraged, Balarama swung his plough, her hair with it, and dragged her towards him. This story brings out the violence associated with canal irrigation. Balarama, who is associated with the pestle and the plough, is clearly the god of agriculture, while Krishna, associated with cows and horses, is the god of animal husbandry. As domesticators of the animal and plant world, Krishna and Balarama personify the primary economic activities of any society.

The undomesticated and the domesticated forms of nature, the forest and the field, represent two forms of the Goddess. The former is Tripura Bhairavi, the most feared goddess in the three worlds, and the latter is Tripura Sundari, the most desired goddess in the three worlds. The Goddess is simultaneously Chandi, frightening, and Lalita, fascinating. Worshippers of Shiva distinguish the undomesticated and the domesticated parts of Brahmanda as Kali and Gauri. The former is wild and bloodthirsty.

The latter is gentle and nourishing. The former drinks blood; the latter gives milk.

Gauri

Gauri, also known as Annapoorni, giver of food, is fair, dressed as a married woman in green sari with green bangles and hair tied in a knot with strings of flowers. Gauri sits on Shiva's left lap, enjoying his attention. In Gauri, sex and violence are contained to satisfy the needs of her family. She is nature domesticated. She is everything that the dark, naked, bloodthirsty Kali is not.

Nature that is tamed by dharma exists outside us as well as inside us. For culture to thrive, the mind needs to be tamed as much as the forest. Taming of the mind involves bridling desire, lust, greed, ambition—all the forces that threaten civilization.

Domestication of the mind involves balancing desire with duty, instinct with intellect, urges with responsibilities. The following narrative describes how Shvetaketu establishes the institution of marriage based on sexual fidelity. Sex is a natural phenomenon but marriage is a social institution. In nature, any man and woman, even father and daughter, can have sexual relations with no fetters controlling their sexual behaviour or the number of sexual partners. In culture, rules define how man and woman should behave sexually. Just as the farmer turns the forest into a field with fences and choice of seed, the husband domesticates the wife through laws of marriage and ensures she bears only his children.

Shvetaketu's Law

Shvetaketu saw his mother in the arms of another man. When he complained to his father he was told, 'All women are free to do as they wish.' Horrified by this statement, Shvetaketu realized that it was thus impossible for any man to know who his biological father was. Shvetaketu was determined to set things right; so he decreed that henceforth a woman could have sexual relations only with her husband or with whoever he selected. (Mahabharata)

The story brings to light the arbitrary nature of social codes. Shvetaketu decrees that a woman shall have sexual relations only with her husband or with whoever he selects. Thus it was possible for a man to become a father without actually impregnating his wife. In society, fatherhood is not necessarily a biological concept; it is a legal status. In the following story, a man becomes a father posthumously simply because, by law, even in death he is master of his wife's womb.

Vichitravirya's Children

Vichitravirya, king of Hastinapur, had two wives, Ambika and Ambalika, but he died before he could father a child. So his mother, Satyavati, requested the sage Vyasa to impregnate the widows. As a result, Ambika became mother of Dhritarashtra and Ambalika mother of Pandu, heirs to the throne of Hastinapur. (Mahabharata)

According to the code of dharma, women had only one duty: obey the father when unmarried, the husband when married and the son when widowed. For men, duty was determined by varna, station in society, and ashrama, the stage in life.

Krishna, the Cowherd

As Krishna, Vishnu identifies himself with the lower stations of society. He is visualized as a cowherd in the first part of his life and as a charioteer in the second half. As a cowherd, he plays the flute and enchants the cows with his music. As charioteer, he wields the whip to bridle horses. Cows represent the earth that nourishes life and need to be treated with respect. Horses represent the mind that threatens social order unless disciplined. Krishna thus domesticates both the outer world (earth) and the inner world (mind).

The Rig Samhita states that the organism that is society has for its head priests and philosophers, who give direction to people. The arms are made up of warriors and administrators, who defend and regulate society. The trunk is made up of merchants and traders involved in wealth generation. The feet are made up of labourers and craftsmen and artisans and entertainers, who live in the service of others. Varna was decided at birth—the son of a priest could only be a priest and he could only marry a member of the same varna. This brought predictability into society.

The ashrama system ensured the old generation made way for the new generation and no two generations milked nature at the same time.

Varna: The Stations of Society

Varna	Role	Part of Society	Need of Society
Brahmana	Priest	Head	Spirituality
Kshatriya	Warrior	Arms	Administration
Vaishya	Merchant	Trunk	Economics
Shudra	Labourer	Feet	Service

Ashrama: The Stages of Life

Ashrama	Role	Aim	Process
Brahmacharya	Student	Preparing for society	Learning
Grihastha	Householder	Member of society	Acquiring
Vanaprastha	Retired	Retiring from society	Sharing
Sanyasa	Hermit	Detached from society	Abandoning

A perfect society is one where varna–ashrama–dharma is upheld perfectly. When this happens, the milestones of life, known as samskaras, follow each other with rhythmic regularity. Life begins with a naming ceremony, followed by the rituals of shaving the hair, piercing the ear, giving the child solid food, teaching the child to read and write, getting the child educated, then married. Marriage is followed by the birth of the next generation. When the new generation comes, the old generation dies. Funeral rites involve the promise to produce children, for through children the forefathers are reborn. This predictability is the hallmark of the perfect society. Rama's kingdom was said to be such a kingdom. The rains always came on time. There were no diseases or accidents. No surprises.

Shambuka Beheaded

In Ayodhya, one day, a boy died. His father, a brahmana, accused Rama of not upholding dharma in his kingdom. Why else would a son die before his father? Rama consulted the sages, who informed him that a shudra by the name of Shambuka was immersed in the ascetic activity known as tapa. The Rishis explained, 'In the age we live in, dharma does not allow shudras to become ascetics. The age when that is permitted is yet to come. Shambuka's action has disturbed the balance of the cosmos. The result is disorder, death of a son before the father.' Rama immediately went to the forest and beheaded Shambuka. Dharma was re-established. Predictable rhythms of nature returned. (Uttara Ramayana)

The Ramayana admits that establishing the law of society is not always superior to the law of the jungle. While nature treats all men and women equally, culture with its code of dharma treats man differently from woman. Among men, some are given more privileges than others. Nature may favour the strong, but culture also has its favourites. Any organization—natural or cultural—has a hierarchy and with hierarchy comes tension.

In the story of Shambuka, Rama is confronted with the darker aspect of the varna system—the caste system that allows certain members of society to have more choices than others. In the following story, Rama faces the greatest challenge of his life: his dharma as a good husband comes into conflict with his dharma as a good king. This story forms the most controversial part of the Ramayana.

◎

The Gold Effigy of Sita

After Rama had killed Ravana, the Rakshasas released Sita. But Rama refused to accept her as his wife until she proved her chastity. Sita stepped into fire; such was her purity that Agni, the fire-god, refused to burn her. With his wife's chastity publicly demonstrated, Rama returned to Ayodhya with Sita by his side. His subjects in Ayodhya, however, refused to accept as their queen a woman of soiled reputation. In deference to the wishes of his people, Rama decided to abandon Sita. She was sent to the forest, where she gave birth to the twin sons of Rama, Luv and Kush. As king, Rama was expected to perform the Ashwamedha yagna. To perform a yagna, a king must have a queen. People requested Rama to remarry. Rama refused: he had abandoned the woman his subjects did not want as their queen but he had never abandoned the woman who was his wife. Eternally faithful to Sita, Rama placed a gold effigy of Sita in the place reserved for the wife, gold being the metal symbolizing purity. As part of the ceremony, the royal horse was released outside the city. All the lands the horse traversed unchallenged came under Rama's suzerainty. The horse moved freely in every direction until it was captured by Luv and Kush. Though mere boys, the twins withstood the attack of Rama's great army and managed to keep the horse captive. That Rama was defeated by two children was a clear indicator that dharma was not on the side of Rama. It was on the side of Sita, the mother of the two boys. Realizing their folly, the people of Ayodhya begged Sita to return as their queen. 'Let them see how pure you are,' said Rama. 'Go through the trial by fire once again.' Sita, tired of proving her chastity repeatedly, decided to prove her purity by a different method. 'If I have thought of no man but Rama as my husband, let the earth split and consume me.' Instantly the earth split open and Sita disappeared under the earth. Everyone got their proof. But the children lost their mother and Rama his wife. Without Sita, Rama could not bear to live on earth. He entered the river Sarayu and did not rise again. (Uttara Ramayana)

Sita's magical powers come from her chastity. Fire does not hurt her; victory always follows her. Even the earth splits at her command. Such is the power of a wife who submits unquestioningly to the code of civilized behaviour, however cruel it may be.

Rama suffers greatly because he has to choose between the dharma of a king and the dharma of a husband. As king, he must respect his people's wishes. As husband, he can never be unfaithful to his wife. In the struggle to balance the two roles, Rama's personal life takes a toll. Rama's poise and dignity in the face of such pressure and tragedy make him, in the eyes of Hindus, the supreme upholder of social values, maryada purushottam.

Descents from Vaikuntha

In this section, the conflict between cultural demands and natural urges is identified as the root of social change and the cause of cultural decay.

Vishnu is always described in royal terms. He resides in his heavenly court, Vaikuntha, located in the middle of the ocean of milk. There he grants audience to all his devotees while reclining on the coils of the thousand-hooded serpent, Sesha, gently swaying on the waves of the ocean. At his feet is his wife Lakshmi, demure and domesticated, massaging his feet.

The god of pleasure, Kama, is said to be the son of Lakshmi. The Apsaras or nymphs are her handmaidens. Dhanvantari, the god of health, is her attendant and a form of Vishnu. Vishnu is thus associated with both spiritual joys and corporeal pleasures. Vishnu temples are invariably opulent. The presiding deity a rasik, the enjoyer of rasa, aesthetic juices of life. Vishnu loves good food, good clothes, good music. With his consort by his side, he sits on swings in springtime, goes on chariot rides in summertime and boat rides on moonlit nights. Vishnu's world is full of rich colours, a rangabhoomi, in which he plays, fully aware of what the world is.

Baby on a Banyan Leaf

Vishnu or Krishna is often visualized as a baby boy sucking his right toe while lying on a banyan leaf cradled by the waves. The waves represent the impermanent nature of life, the banyan leaf the permanent presence of God. The baby is the symbol of renewal, its male gender indicative of the soul. The left and lower halves of the body represent material delights while the right and upper halves represent spiritual bliss. By sucking the right toe, the gurgling, delightful child invites all jivas to experience both the material delights and the spiritual bliss found in samsara without getting overwhelmed by its impermanent nature.

Lakshmi is generally regarded as a fickle goddess. Like wealth she is whimsical, constantly on the move. No one knows in which direction she will go. That she always resides at Vishnu's feet is an indicator that she is drawn by dharma. With dharma comes order; with order comes peace. Peace ushers in prosperity. With prosperity comes power. Prosperity and power patronize the arts. Arts are associated with Saraswati.

In many temples Saraswati also is treated as Vishnu's consort. Saraswati resides on his tongue and Lakshmi at his feet. These two wives constantly quarrel with each other. Wealth believes it makes the world go round; knowledge believes it makes the world worth living. As king of the cosmos, Vishnu needs both wealth and wisdom, Lakshmi and Saraswati. Knowledge is a faithful wife. Saraswati is difficult to acquire, but once she comes into a person's life she never leaves. Wealth, on the other hand, is a demanding wife. Lakshmi comes and goes as she pleases and one must constantly strive to keep her coming. Knowledge does not outlive death. Wealth does. Distribution of knowledge only enhances it. Distribution of wealth depletes it. The difference between Saraswati and Lakshmi is apparent in their respective symbols.

Lakshmi has two forms: Bhoodevi and Shridevi. The former is the goddess of earth, the latter the goddess of heaven. The former is associated with fertility, the latter with glory and power. The former bestows tangible wealth in the form of gold and grain. The latter bestows intangible wealth: power, fame and

Table Lakshmi and Saraswati

Lakshmi	Saraswati
She is bejewelled, as a bride	She wears no jewels, like a widow
Wears red sari, associated with fertility	Wears white sari, associated with spirituality
Holds in her hands pots, pans and lotus flowers, indicative of household chores	Holds in her hands books and musical instruments, indicative of intellectual pursuits
Rides an elephant, symbol of royal power	Rides a heron, symbol of concentration
Associated with gold, symbol of affluence	Associated with crystal, symbol of clarity

glory. Bhoodevi is a gentle, nurturing wife content to serve her husband. Shridevi is restless; Vishnu has to constantly struggle to keep her happy. If Vishnu is king, Bhoodevi is his kingdom and Shridevi his crown, his sceptre, his throne, his parasol and his royal yak-tail fly whisk.

When all is well in the world, there is a consistency and predictability in natural and cultural rhythms. There are no surprises or accidents. The world looks good. At such times, Vishnu reclines on his serpent-couch in Vaikuntha and a discus whirrs round his index finger. This is the Sudarshan chakra. Sudarshan means a positive outlook. The chakra's whirring round God's right index finger is indicative of rhythmic order.

In his left hand, Vishnu holds the Panchajanya, the conch-shell trumpet, blown at the time of war, blown to keep troublemakers at bay. The conch has a spiral shape, indicating that the rhythm of society is not merely repetitive but also spiral, winding up and down over time. Despite the stability offered by dharma, Vishnu cannot stop the march of time. Just as a disciplined existence ensures health but does not prevent ageing and death, Vishnu's dharma ensures stability in society but does not prevent the gradual ageing of society.

By giving society a head, arms, feet and trunk, the Rig Samhita effectively personifies it, and transforms it into a living organism, one that responds to circumstances, one that transforms over time. Like every organism, society has a finite period of existence. A society's lifespan is known as kalpa; it comprises four eras, or yugas, which represent the childhood, youth, maturity and senility of society. Desires in each phase are different. So are concepts of order.

Table Four Eras of the Society

	Quarter	Yuga	Phase of the Cosmos	Reproductive Activity	Means to Acquire Wealth	Number of Legs of the Bull of Order
Kalpa	First	Krita	Childhood	Thought	Charity	Four
	Second	Treta	Youth	Touch	Force	Three
	Third	Dvapara	Maturity	Intercourse	Trickery	Two
	Fourth	Kali	Senility	Perverted	Exploitation	One
Pralaya			Death			

If dharma is represented by a bull, it would have four, three and two legs in the Krita, Treta and Dvapara yugas and one leg in the Kali yuga before it is swept away by pralaya, death of the world before its rebirth. Clearly then the childhood of society, like the childhood of man, is a much desired state. We may yearn for it all our lives, but it will never last forever.

Every time dharma is threatened Vishnu mounts his eagle, the mighty Garuda, and comes to earth ready to do battle. The descents of Vishnu from Vaikuntha to earth are his avatars or incarnations. The form in each descent is different because the demands of the world each time are different. The different avatars thus reinforce the idea that rules and regulations that maintain order are not static by nature. They are forged when the demands of desire clash with the quest for order. As man's understanding of the world changes, desires change and so do concepts of order. Rules have to therefore constantly adapt themselves. Social stability must not be compromised, yet new ideas must be respected. Vishnu's descents are not just about re-establishing order. It is also about redefining them.

Matsya	Fish that rescues Veda, plants and animals
Kurma	Turtle that supports the churn to obtain treasures dissolved in the ocean of milk
Varaha	Boar that raises the earth from the bottom of the sea
Narasimha	Man-lion who defies classification and overpowers mortals who seek to outwit death
Vamana	Dwarf who claims the sky for the Devas and shoves the Asuras below the surface of the earth
Parashurama	Priest who turns to violence to kill unrighteous kings and unchaste women
Rama	King who upholds old rules at the cost of personal life
Krishna	Cowherd/charioteer/statesman who shrewdly changes rules
Buddha	Teacher who propagates monasticism
Kalki	Revolutionary who dismantles the world

The Cycle of Incarnations

Each avatar of Vishnu involves a crisis involving the Goddess. Vishnu takes the form of a turtle to help the Devas churn Lakshmi out, the form of a boar to rescue the earth that has been dragged under the sea, the form of Rama when Sita is abducted and the form of Krishna to help Draupadi. Thus the Goddess is the embodiment of nature and culture. She is the kingdom and Vishnu is the king. She is Bhoodevi and he is Bhoopati. She is Shridevi and he is Shripati. Both validate each other, she by giving him powers of kingship and he by defending her.

It is through kings that Vishnu ensures dharma is upheld on earth. In the following narrative, Bhoodevi begs Vishnu to rescue her from irresponsible kings who, rather than instituting and maintaining varna–ashrama–dharma in their respective kingdoms, indulge their ambition and greed, usurp neighbouring kingdoms by brute force and plunder the earth's resources. This not only disturbs social order, it also threatens the balance between nature and culture.

The Cries of Bhoodevi

Bhoodevi once went to Vaikuntha in the form of a cow. She had tears in her eyes. 'My back is broken and my udders are sore. The kings of earth plunder my wealth. Help me, my lord.' Vishnu wiped her tears and promised to descend on earth as Parashurama, Rama and Krishna and repair the damage caused by kings. In gratitude, Bhoodevi saluted Vishnu as Govinda, the guardian of the earth-cow. (Bhagavata Purana)

The shift from Krita yuga to Dvapara yuga happens when a king abandons charity and abuses his military might for personal gain. To restore order, Vishnu descends as Parashurama.

Parashurama

Parashurama is a priest by birth who chooses to become a warrior to fight and destroy unjust kings. Thus social order collapses when kings and leaders abandon dharma in their quest for power. Even God acknowledges this.

The Theft of Jamadagni's Cow

Vishnu had given Kiratavirya-arjuna a thousand arms.
Kiratavirya had used these arms to establish a prosperous
kingdom, where he invited many sages to perform
yagna. One of these sages was Jamadagni, whom
he gifted the sacred cow Nandini. Later, Kiratavirya
discovered that Nandini was a magical cow; from its
udders it could provide food to feed an army. He decided
to take the cow back. This was against dharma. Jamadagni
tried to appeal to the king's sense of duty but the king
dragged the cow away. Jamadagni's youngest son,
Parashurama, could not bear the king's behaviour. He
raised an axe, chased the king and hacked his arms to
pieces, causing him to bleed to death. He then returned
to his father's hermitage with the cow. The king's sons
decided to avenge their father's death. They rode into
Jamadagni's hermitage and killed him in front of his wife.
Infuriated, Parashurama took a vow to exterminate five
generations of the warrior clan and make his funeral
offerings to his father in blood. It was a vow he fulfilled
with a ruthlessness that horrified the whole world.
(Bhagavata Purana)

Parashurama also kills his mother for being unfaithful to his father,
and his brothers for disobeying their father. Parashurama thus
represents Vishnu's outrage at the collapse of order. When kings
do not uphold dharma, when husbands and wives are not faithful

to each other, when sons do not obey their father, nothing can be predicted in life. In a society where things are not predictable nothing in manageable.

The Beheading of Renuka

Renuka had the ability to collect water in unbaked pots by the power of her chastity. One day, however, she saw a gandharva bathing in the river and felt sexually attracted to him. This moment of infidelity took away her magical powers. When her husband learned of this, he ordered his sons to behead her. His eldest four refused to do so. But Parashurama obeyed without question. He raised his axe and severed her head from her body. Jamadagni then ordered his son to kill his elder brothers because by disobeying their father they had not been true to dharma. Parashurama killed his brothers too. Much pleased, Jamadagni asked his son for a boon. 'Give me back my mother and brothers,' said Parashurama. 'So be it,' replied the father. (Bhagavata Purana)

Like Sita, Renuka has magical powers until adulterous thoughts creep into her heart. By itself, sexual desire between man and woman is never inappropriate. In fact, as in the following story, nature does not discourage it even when culture deems it incestuous. Ideas such as incest and adultery are based on social values. They make no sense in the natural world.

The Curse of Urvashi

Arjuna once paid a visit to Indra's court. Such was his beauty that the Apsara Urvashi desired him greatly. She offered herself to him freely. 'I cannot touch you as you were once the wife of my ancestor, Pururava,' said Arjuna, reminding Urvashi that as Apsara her lifespan was much longer than his. 'Rules of your society do not apply to nymphs such as me,' said Urvashi. She demanded that Arjuna satisfy her. Arjuna refused. The idea of incest horrified him. Furious, Urvashi cursed that Arjuna would lose his manhood. Indra modified the curse and Arjuna suffered emasculation for only one year. During that year he lived like a palace eunuch called Brihanalla in the court of Virata. (Mahabharata)

Emotions are the greatest threat to the order imposed by dharma. Sexual desire, ambition, anger, hatred and even love threaten the rigid boundaries of varna and ashrama. Vishnu himself contributes to it when as Parashurama, in righteous indignation, he abandons the priestly ways of his family and picks up an axe and behaves like a warrior. This marks the beginning of an eventual, inevitable collapse.

In the incarnation that follows Parashurama, towards the end of the Treta yuga, this error is rectified. Rama is born into a royal family and he behaves all his life as prescribed by his station in society. Even in the forest, he behaves like a king. He may have been forced out of civilization but civilization is never forced out of him. But in Rama, there seems to be an almost absence of emotion. In the quest to uphold order, he sacrifices his feelings. He suffers silently. All for the rule. This makes dharma, however noble in intent, an extremely insufferable idea.

After the incarnation of Rama, Vishnu descends as Krishna. He is born in the Dvapara yuga, when the laws of marriage do not demand monogamy as in the time of Rama. Men have many wives and women have many husbands. The Pandavas have the same mother but different biological fathers. Arjuna, the third Pandava, has Draupadi, Uloopi, Chitrangada and Subhadra for his wives. And he shares Draupadi with his four brothers. It is a time when nobody respects varna; people do not respect their station in society. Thus the teacher of the Pandavas, Drona, though born a priest, lives like a warrior and king. It is also a time when fathers are willing to destroy the youth of their children for their own pleasures. In the following story, Yadu is the ancestor of the Yadavas.

The Curse of Yayati

When Devayani learned that her husband, Yayati, had secretly married her maid Sarmishtha and that the maid had borne him two sons, Devayani ran to her father, the Asura-priest Shukra, who cursed that Yayati would become old and impotent. When he realized the implications of the curse, Shukra modified it, stating that Yayati would regain his youth and potency if one of his sons willingly bore the burden of the curse. The eldest son, Yadu, refused to suffer the curse. The youngest son, Puru, agreed to become old and impotent so that his father could enjoy life. When Yayati had had his fill of pleasures, he blessed Puru and made him king, even though he was the youngest and born of the maid. Yadu, eldest son of the chief queen, was cursed by Yayati that neither he nor his descendants would ever be king. (Mahabharata)

Krishna is born into the family of Yadavas and because of Yayati's curse can never be king, only kingmaker. Many psychologists believe this story captures the Indian psyche quite accurately wherein the younger generation is lauded for sacrificing its happiness to satisfy the demands of the older generation.

Krishna is witness to a crisis between model social codes and unreasonable aspirations of the people. Krishna acknowledges, suffers and resolves this conflict between head and heart with compassion and love. Surrounded by social turbulence, he remains calm and composed, with an endearing look in his eyes and a smile on his lips. This makes him poorna-avatar, the complete and most perfect incarnation of God.

Both the Ramayana, which tells the story of Rama, and the Mahabharata, which tells the story of Krishna, are concerned with the struggle between the law of the jungle and the code of civilization. In one, Ravana represents the desire to dominate society by force. In the other, this role is taken up by the Kauravas. In one, the abduction of Sita marks the collapse of civil society. In the other, this happens when Draupadi is gambled away and disrobed in public. But while in the Ramayana Rama does not contribute to the abduction of Sita, in the Mahabharata the gambling away and disrobing of Draupadi are the direct results of her husbands' loss of control over good sense.

The Disrobing of Draupadi

The Kauravas invited the five Pandava brothers to a game of dice. During the game, the Pandavas gambled away everything they possessed, even their kingdom, Indraprastha. Yudhishtira, who represented his brothers, in a desperate bid to win back all he lost, staked his brothers and then himself. He lost each time. Finally, he gambled away their common wife, Draupadi. The Kauravas, ecstatic in victory, dragged Draupadi to the gambling hall and decided to assert their authority over her and her husbands by disrobing her in public. As they did so, Draupadi raised her arms in helplessness. Krishna heard her cry and every yard of cloth that was removed by the Kauravas was magically replaced by another cloth. (Mahabharata)

Draupadi's humiliation is witnessed by all the kings of the earth. But none step forward to help her. There are hair-splitting arguments on whether it is within the purview of dharma to do so. In other words, no king finds anything obviously terrible in a woman being dragged and disrobed in public. This dramatic episode draws attention to the tragedy of laws that in their dispassionate execution forget the reason dharma exists in the first place: to enable the weak to thrive. There can be no order in a society where the law permits kings to gamble away their kingdoms and husbands to gamble away their wives. When the letter of the law becomes more important than the spirit of the law, when rules matter more than people, when order is established without compassion, it is time to re-examine dharma.

If the earth is the Goddess, clothed she is the domesticated, nourishing mother and wife; unclothed she is the wild, untamed goddess. Clothed she gives milk. Unclothed she demands blood. The disrobing of Draupadi is a visual representation of the collapse of order. The rise of the law of the jungle. Draupadi responds as Kali, refusing to tie her hair until she washes it in the blood of the Kauravas. Nothing will establish order until the blood of the Kauravas quenches the earth's quest for justice.

Kali

Kali's bloodthirsty, naked and unbound form is indicative of the wild and raw state of the Goddess when God is indifferent to her. Kali represents nature, the darkest recesses of the unconsciousness that can overwhelm culture when discipline gives way to desire and the social fabric collapses.

The Pandavas agree to go into forest exile for thirteen years, at the end of which the Kauravas agree to return them their kingdom. Since the Pandavas brought this upon themselves, their exile seems a fitting punishment. Rama's exile by contrast is imposed upon him by his ambitious stepmother, Kaikeyi. Unfortunately for Kaikeyi, her son, Bharata, rejects the kingdom obtained through foul play. He is more than eager to return the kingdom to his brother on his return from exile. The Kauravas, on the other hand, refuse to do so. By going back on their word, the Kauravas once again demonstrate they follow the law of the barbarians, not the law of culture. Krishna then leads the Pandavas into the battlefield of Kurukshetra and does everything to ensure the Kauravas' defeat.

The Defeat of the Kauravas

The Kaurava army was first led by Bhisma, who could not be killed so long as he held a bow in his hand. He would never raise a bow against a woman but women were not allowed into the battlefield. Knowing this, Krishna made Shikhandi ride on Arjuna's chariot. Shikhandi had been born with a woman's body but later in life acquired a man's body. According to Bhisma, Shikhandi was still a woman. According to Krishna, he was not. Bhisma refused to shoot arrows at Shikhandi. Behind Shikhandi stood Arjuna, who took advantage of Bhisma's decision and shot a hundred arrows through Bhisma's body as soon as the latter lowered his bow.

After Bhisma fell, the Kaurava army was led by Drona. Drona was extremely attached to his son, Ashwathama. So Krishna made Yudhishtira, who had never spoken a lie, tell Drona that Ashwathama was dead. 'You will be referring to a dead elephant but he will think it is his son. In sorrow he will put down his weapons,' said Krishna.

Drona behaved predictably. As soon as he lowered his bow, Krishna ordered Draupadi's brother to behead him.

Then the Kaurava army was led by Karna. Just when Karna came face to face with Arjuna the wheel of his chariot got stuck in the ground. 'Dharma demands that warriors face each other on equal terms. Wait till I release this wheel,' said Karna as he jumped from his chariot and tried to pull out the wheel. While his back was turned, Krishna told Arjuna to shoot the fatal arrow. 'Dharma does not apply to one who did not feel the disrobing of Draupadi was against dharma,' argued Krishna. Finally, when the rest of the Kauravas were dead, Bhima challenged Duryodhana to a duel. Both were experts in the use of the mace, and in the fight that followed it was clear that both were equally matched. Krishna then signalled to Bhima to hit Duryodhana below his waist and break his thigh. This was against the rules of civilized warfare. But it was done. Everybody condemned Krishna but, with the defeat of the Kauravas and the coronation of Yudhishtira, a new social order came into being, one in which might was not right. (Mahabharata)

A comparison of the Ramayana and the Mahabharata shows that, though both seek to establish order in the world, they are clearly responses to different needs. The Ramayana is about compliance; the Mahabharata is about revolution. Rama strives to keep old rules; Krishna struggles to make new rules. Rama's approach, unfortunately, allows for the exile of Sita. Krishna's approach is marked by a furious bloodbath, where all rules of civilized warfare are disregarded.

What is dharma for Rama can never be dharma for Krishna because Rama and Krishna belong to different points in time. Rama resides in an earlier, purer age and Krishna in a later, darker age. As the Manu Smriti states, rules and regulations need to change with time and space; they need to respond to history and adapt to geography.

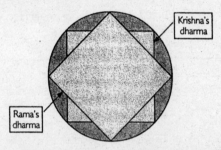

The Changing Squares within the Circle

Table Comparison of the Epics Ramayana and Mahabharata

Ramayana	Mahabharata
Rama obeys his father without question	Yadu, Krishna's ancestor, does not obey his father
Rama never kills a relative	Krishna kills his maternal uncle, avenging the death of his six brothers
There is no division of the kingdom	The kingdom is divided between the Pandavas and the Kauravas
Rama's father has three wives only because none are able to help him father sons, and Rama has only one wife, Sita	Krishna has many wives and the Pandavas too; the five brothers also share a common wife, Draupadi
Rama protects his wife, Sita, and kills Ravana, who abducts her	The Pandavas gamble away their wife and stand helplessly aside while she is publicly disrobed by the Kauravas
Rama never breaks the rules while fighting Ravana	The Pandavas, led by Krishna, break many rules while fighting the Kauravas

Hindus are advised against reading the Mahabharata inside their homes for fear that ideas in that book, such as brothers fighting over property, will pollute family values. They prefer reading the Ramayana because in it brothers never fight over inheritance. The principle underlying this custom is known as 'sympathetic or imitative magic', according to which events in a household are influenced by the ideas expressed in sacred symbols and rituals and narratives. That is why during marriage and childbirth

Table   Symbols of Affluence

Symbol	Reason
Gold jewels	Because gold cannot be destroyed and ornaments represent celebration of life
Piles of sweets	Because they represent abundance of all things desirable
Banana plant	Because it regenerates itself and does not require cultivation
Coconut	Because every part of the plant has an economic value
Stalks of rice grain	Because they represent food, and a place where there is abundant water
Betel nut and leaves	Because they are chewed after an enjoyable meal to help relax and digest the food
Mango leaves	Because the succulent fruit makes the heat of summer bearable
Marigold flowers	Because each petal has a seed that can give rise to a marigold plant
Butter	Because it is churned from milk and cream
Sugar cane	Because its sap is sweet and juicy
Flowers	Because they are colourful and fragrant, arousing the senses
Sandal paste	Because it is cool and fragrant
Lamps	Because they take away the darkness
Incense	Because they make the environment fragrant

symbols associated with fruition and fertility and opulence are placed in all corners of the house.

The same logic that prohibits the reading of the Mahabharata in the house also prescribes the reading of stories from the Bhagavata. The Bhagavata literature describes Krishna's childhood before he came into contact with the Pandavas.

The Bhagavata and the Mahabharata present two different Krishnas. The Bhagavata describes the first half of Krishna's life and the Mahabharata the final half of Krishna's life. In the former, Krishna is a cowherd, who plays the flute and dances with milkmaids. In the latter, Krishna is a kingmaker, who establishes cities and rides chariots into battlefields. The Bhagavata is full of innocence, adventure and romance. The Mahabharata is full of intrigue, politics and philosophy. In

Table Comparison of Two Krishnas

Krishna of Vrindavana	Krishna of Dwarka
A mischievous and romantic rake	A shrewd strategist
Appeals to the heart	Appeals to the head
Rural setting	Urban setting
Enchants cows with the music of his flute	Controls horses with his whip
Lover of 16,108 milkmaids	Husband of 16,108 queens
Protects the village from natural calamities, such as forest fires and torrential rains, and dangerous animals	Establishes cities and protects them from ambitious kings, such as Jarasandha and Shalva
Leaves the village with a promise to return	Is cursed to die after witnessing the collapse of his city and death of his family
Associated with milk and romance	Associated with blood and war

both, Krishna is associated with 16,108 women. In the Bhagavata, these women are simple milkmaids who love him unconditionally and who engage with him on purely emotional terms. In the Mahabharata, these women are princesses who also love him unconditionally, but they engage with him in purely social terms. For the milkmaids, Krishna is the beloved. For the princesses, Krishna is husband.

Krishna and Radha

Radha is not Krishna's wife. Yet without her image, Krishna is never complete. She inspires him to play the flute. Without her, there is no music. In some traditions she is considered Krishna's aunt. In others she is married to another man. In most she is older than him. Thus the love of Radha and Krishna defies all social norms. Their meeting, when they are surrounded by a circle of dancing milkmaids, the Maha-Raas, always takes place at night, outside the village, in secret. It represents the desires of the heart that unfortunately have to be denied or repressed or sublimated by the demands of society. Though denied, repressed and sublimated, they exist. And Krishna acknowledges their existence.

The Mahabharata unfolds a world of men—of warriors and priests. The Bhagavata is a world of women—lovers and mothers. Krishna has two mothers. His biological mother is Devaki, who has to give him up at birth so that he can be raised in secret in the village of cowherds away from the murderous hands of her brother, Kamsa, the dictator of Mathura, whom Krishna is destined to kill. Devaki belongs to Mathura, the city. Krishna is raised in a village, Gokul, by Yashoda, wife of the chief of cowherds. Most songs identify Krishna both as Devaki's son and as Yashoda's son. One is left to wonder if Krishna is Krishna because he is of noble birth or because of his humble upbringing. Is it nature or culture which defines him? One is also reminded that relationships can be forged not just by blood but also by emotions.

The Mahabharata Krishna is associated with blood. The Bhagavata Krishna is associated with milk and butter. Butter is made by churning the cream of milk. Krishna loves butter. He pesters his mother for it. He steals it from the dairies much to the exasperation of the milkmaids. For Vishnu who reclines on the ocean of milk, this butter clearly represents the best that life has to offer. The butter is Shridevi, the delight of material existence. The butter is Radha, who loves unconditionally. The cow who gives this butter is the earth itself, Bhoodevi. This Bhoodevi begs for protection from kings who plunder and abuse her. And so the cowherd Krishna of the Bhagavata transforms into the charioteer Krishna of the Mahabharata, orchestrates the slaughter of kings who do not uphold dharma and nourishes the earth with their blood. Draupadi is the blood-seeking Bhoodevi, abused by the Kauravas and betrayed by the Pandavas. Helpless, she seeks Krishna. Only by stepping out of the Bhagavata and entering the Mahabharata can Vishnu fulfil his role as Govinda, guardian of the earth-cow.

Eventually, inevitably, society ages. And Vishnu's avatars cannot reverse or stem the decay. A time comes when Vishnu is too tired to fight. He needs to sleep. For that to happen, society must be dismantled. The final incarnations of Vishnu are associated not with preservation but with closure.

In the following story, Vishnu is no longer the God who affirms worldly life; he conspires to bring down three cities inhabited by the Asuras—in other words, three worlds inhabited by souls who have moved so far away from the param-atma that they need to be destroyed. The Asuras follow the Veda, but they use its wisdom to dominate the outer world rather than to discover the inner true self. Vishnu therefore draws them away from the Veda. That he plays the role of a monk and that he is helped by Shiva, the ascetic form of God, suggest that, in the Hindu world view, world-renunciation is as good as world-destruction. Significantly, the very elements used by Vishnu to churn the wonders of the world from the ocean of milk—Meru and Sesha—are used by Shiva as the shaft of his bow and the bowstring to shoot down the three cities. Vishnu himself serves as the arrow.

The Three Cities

Three Asuras had obtained a boon that enabled them to build three flying cities. These cities travelled between the three worlds, causing havoc. Desperate, the Devas turned to Brahma. Brahma revealed that the cities could be destroyed only if they were struck by a single arrow. This could happen only if the cities were aligned in a single line and the arrow was shot by a divine archer. Shiva was the chosen archer. Meru was the shaft of his bow and Sesha his bowstring. The earth was his chariot; the sun and the moon were its wheels. Brahma was the charioteer and the four books of the Veda were his horses. Shiva waited for the cities to align in a single line. But the cities kept flying in different directions, such was their will to survive. Vishnu then took the form of a monk and visited the three cities and taught the Asuras the doctrine of renunciation. Eventually, the Asuras lost all interest in worldly life. They did not bother to fly their cities in different directions. The cities aligned in a single line. At that moment, Shiva drew his great bow. Vishnu served as his arrow. Shiva released the arrow and Vishnu pierced all three cities, destroying them in an instant. Shiva smeared his body with the ash of the cities—three horizontal lines. (Shiva Purana)

Ash is the symbol of the soul: that which survives even when the three worlds are destroyed. Vishnu as Shiva's arrow liberates the soul of the Asuras entrapped by their demonic bodies. Shiva uses this ash to smear his body. Unlike Vishnu, who celebrates the flesh by adorning it with silk and sandal paste, Shiva gives attention only to the soul. This shift in attention marks the end of worldly life.

Vishnu, the Monk

According to the Skanda Purana, Vishnu took the form of a hermit and taught the Asuras a monastic doctrine; this caused the Asuras to lose power and be defeated by the Devas. In the *Gita Govinda*, there is a different explanation for the monk-incarnation of Vishnu. He took the form of a pacifist monk to stop animal sacrifices. The former story is a strategic narrative aimed at showing monastic orders such as Buddhism in a poor light. The latter story is an attempt to incorporate Buddhism into the Hindu fold.

Kalki

Kalki is the final incarnation of Vishnu in the lifetime of every world. He rides a white horse and swings a gleaming sword and dismantles a world where dharma has collapsed.

Finally as Kalki, Vishnu rides his horse and sets about destroying the whole world with his sharp sword. When all is done, he withdraws into a dreamless slumber, and the sea rises, dissolving nature and culture. It is the hour of pralaya. Nothing is destroyed though. Everything is absorbed into Vishnu's body. For he is the protector, the sustainer, the preserver of all things. All possibilities of life will stay there until it is time for Vishnu to wake up and the world to be reborn.

Matsya

After finishing his duties as king, Satyavrata lived a quiet life with his wife on the banks of a river. Once while bathing in the river he came upon a little fish who could speak. 'Save me from the big fish, O mighty king, and I will save the world.' Feeling sorry for the small fish who talked big, Satyavrata took it out of the river and gave it shelter in his pot. The next day, the fish had grown in size. It did not fit in the pot. So the fish had to be moved to a large urn. As the days passed, the fish kept growing in size. Satyavrata had to move it from the large urn to a pond, from the pond to a river and from the river to the sea. As the fish went across the ocean, beyond the horizon, it told Satyavrata, 'Soon the heavens will burst and torrential rains will flood the earth. The sea will rise and submerge the land. When this happens collect the seed of every plant and a pair of every animal and wait for me on a boat with your wife.' Realizing this was no ordinary fish, but Vishnu himself, Satyavrata did as he was told. The great fish appeared before him, bigger than before, with a horn on its head. Satyavrata tied his boat to the horn with Adi Sesha as the rope. The fish then towed the boat through the great deluge to the only piece of dry land, the peak of Mount Mandara. There Satyavrata and his wife waited for the waters to recede. With the seed of every plant and a pair of all animals he would establish the new world. (Bhagavata Purana)

Everything in the Hindu world is reborn. Men die and are reborn. Societies die and are reborn. The cosmos dies and is reborn. Everything goes and comes back.

Rama's Ring

At the appointed hour, it was time for Rama to die. But Yama, the god of death, could not enter Rama's city, as Hanuman, the mighty monkey, guarded its gates. Hanuman loved Rama so much that he did not want him to die. To distract Hanuman and to let nature take its course, Rama dropped his ring into a crack on the floor and asked Hanuman to fetch the ring. The crack led Hanuman to a subterranean realm, where he found countless copies of Rama's ring. The guardian of the subterranean realm, the serpent-king Vasuki, explained, 'Whenever a ring falls here, a monkey follows it and we know it is time for a Rama to die. Such rings have fallen from above for as long as I can remember, and will continue to do so in the future. As long as the wheel of existence rotates, old worlds die and new ones are reborn. In each world there will be a Hanuman, a Rama and a Rama's ring.' (Ramayana)

Life whirrs like the discus around Vishnu's index finger. The world winds and unwinds like the spiral of his conch.

3
The Point of Shiva and Shakti

In which the soul is realized and matter validated

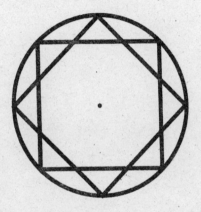

The dimensionless point is the most elemental of geometrical forms. Without the point no circle can be drawn and no square constructed. The dot best represents the soul, the formless divine within us. Just as the existence of a circle presupposes the existence of the centre point, the existence of the world presupposes the existence of a witness to the world—the soul.

Shiva

Shiva is God visualized as an ascetic. Hair matted, body smeared with ash, he sits naked atop a snow-clad mountain, totally internalized, unmindful of the universe around. His phallus is erect but his eyes are shut, indicating that Shiva is aroused not by the delights of the world outside but by the serenity of the soul inside.

Seasons come and go. Cultures rise and fall. Values change. Standards change. Worldly truths seem conditional, relative to space, time and the opinions of people. Shiva is God who is not interested in these worldly truths. He seeks sat, truth that is permanent, absolute, unconditional. So he shuts his eyes to the world, refusing to let memories, desires, ideas and ego crumple his consciouness. Purification of the chitta leads to enlightenment. With enlightenment comes ananda, tranquil bliss. In bliss, Shiva transcends all desires. There is no urge to sense or respond. There is no need for the body or the world. There is no action, no reaction or response. No karma, hence no samsara. The world ceases to be. All that exists is the atma, the uncrumpled pure soul, in self-contained isolation. Shiva is therefore God who destroys the world.

One is a sterile number. When there is only one there can be no love, no yearning, no union. Two are required to forge a relationship. Without the other, the self has no meaning. For sat to make sense there is need for maya, conditional worldly truths. For the stillness of the soul to make sense there is need for the restlessness of energy. The Goddess is Maya, embodiment of all delusions. She is Shakti, personification of energy. She is Adi, primal, as ancient and boundless as the soul. Depending on time, space and judgements of people she can be as wild and fearsome as Kali or as gentle and affectionate as Gauri. She is the world Shiva shuts himself from. She will stir love in his heart, make him open his eyes and be part of worldly life. Love will connect the divine inside with the divine outside. The yearning and union that follow will validate all of existence.

Durga

The embodiment of Adi–Maya–Shakti, Durga is the invincible one. She is at once bride and warrior. The one establishes home, provides pleasure, produces children and offers food. The other rides into battle and kills—defending those who submit to her, destroying those who challenge her. She will tame and ride the lion, the lord of the jungle. Her hair will never be bound.

Fire-Ascetics and Water-Nymphs

In this section, the tension between the stillness of the soul and the restlessness of matter is acknowledged.

If the inner reality of Purusha is best represented by male forms and if the outer reality of Prakriti is best represented by female forms, it follows that sex is the most appropriate metaphor to establish a relationship between them. The recurring theme of 'spilling semen' indicates the spirit's acknowledgement of and interaction with the material world. Refusal to do so indicates the reverse, disconnection between Purusha and Prakriti. The former is creative and fertile. The latter is dangerous, destructive.

The Devas are ever-willing to shed their semen and create new life. They are indifferent to the social consequences of their actions. In the following story, for example, it does not matter to them that the girl asking them to impregnate her is not married. What matters to them is that by making her pregnant they help in rebirth and the rotation of the wheel of samsara. Society is a creation of man, not the gods. In nature, sex is not judged; ideas such as marriage and incest are cultural, born of man-made laws that seek to regulate and control sex, making it acceptable only under certain conditions. The Devas concern themselves with the production of new life, not its legitimacy.

Kunti's Children

As a young girl, Kunti served the sage Durvasa so well that he gave her a mantra, a magical formula, by which she could call upon any god and have a son by him. Kunti used the mantra to call upon Surya, the sun-god. He appeared before her and made her pregnant, even though she was not married. In fear of society, the unmarried Kunti abandoned her child as soon as he was born. After marriage, Kunti's husband, Pandu, was unable to make her pregnant. With his permission, she used her mantra to call upon Yama, Vayu and Indra, gods of order, wind and rain, and have three sons by them. She then gave the formula to Pandu's other wife, Madri, who called upon the Ashwini twins, the celestial physicians, who gave her twin sons: the handsome Nakula and the oracle Sahadeva. (Mahabharata)

According to Tantrik physiology, the dead are reborn when the white seed of man successfully merges with the red seed of woman. Spilt semen holds the possibility of a new life. Spilt menstrual fluid indicates failure to create that life. Seed, white or red, is thus the most potent substance in nature.

White, the colour of male reproductive fluid, represents Purusha; red, the colour of female reproductive fluid, represents Prakriti. The earth is red before the rains. After the rains, the earth is green. Red thus represents the virginal Prakriti who holds the promise of creating new life. Green represents the maternal Prakriti who has realized that promise and created new life. Men and women, such as monks and widows, who seek Purusha and withdraw from worldly life prefer wearing white clothes. Men and women who seek to celebrate the union of Purusha and Prakriti and enjoy worldly life prefer coloured clothes: red for brides, green for mothers.

Semen, menstrual fluid and water, all are forms of rasa. Rasa is the fuel of life, the juice of existence. Rasa flows when God opens his eyes to see the Goddess. It is utilized every time the sense organs and action organs are put to use. Rasa makes the jiva aware of the world. Rasa is required to respond to worldly stimuli.

In its simplest form rasa is water. Rasa is also present in organic minerals. Plants convert rasa in water and minerals into food. In the body, food is converted to blood, flesh, bones, nerves and finally seed. When the white seed of man joins the red seed of woman, a new life is created. Just as the flow of semen creates new life in the womb, the flow of water creates new life on land. In narratives, the flow of semen is used to explain the concept of rasa. In rituals, water is used for the same purpose.

The ritual known as yagna is aimed at promoting the flow of rasa in a particular direction—that of the patron of the yagna—so that it enriches and empowers the patron's life. The Puranas inform us that Daksha, son of Brahma, chief patron of yagna, offers his daughters to the Devas. These daughters of Daksha are, like the daughter of Brahma, symbols of Daksha's world. The Devas fertilize these 'material worlds', make them fruitful and bountiful, much to the delight of Daksha. In the following narrative, Daksha is angry when the moon-god Chandra favours only one of his daughters, letting the others menstruate. He curses that Chandra would lose his virility. Chandra is rescued by Shiva,

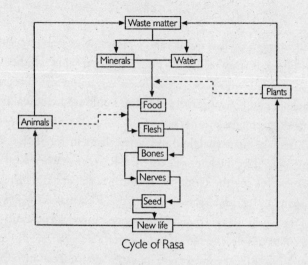

Cycle of Rasa

a form of God that is indifferent to the flow of rasa and uninterested in shedding semen.

Waxing of the Moon

Daksha gave twenty-seven of his daughters in marriage to Chandra, the moon-god, who was renowned for his beauty and virility. Chandra preferred the beautiful Rohini to the others. The neglected wives complained to Daksha, who threatened Chandra with dire consequences if he did not treat all his wives with equal affection, as is expected of any polygamous man. Chandra disregarded Daksha's threat. So he was cursed with a degenerative disease. As the days passed, he lost his potency, and began to wane. A terrified Chandra went to Shiva, who let Chandra sit on his head. There, Chandra found the power to regenerate himself:

his potency returned and he began to wax. A sobered Chandra decided to devote at least one night to each of his twenty-seven wives. And so it is that the moon waxes on the days he approaches Rohini and wanes on the days he moves farther from her. On the new moon night he has no wife by his side. On the day before, when he is just a crescent, the moon celebrates Shiva-ratri, the night of Shiva, and takes refuge on Shiva's locks, safe in the knowledge that he will wax once more. (Somanath Sthala Purana)

Shiva sits still with his eyes firmly shut, unresponsive to any worldly stimuli. His sense and action organs are in a state of total suspension. He does not use even a drop of rasa. Thus retained in his body, semen, hence rasa, transforms into tapa. Tapa is fire. It is ignited the moment God shuts his eyes to the Goddess. Tapa and rasa are in essence the same thing: tapa, the product of separation; rasa, the product of union. By sitting on Shiva's head, Chandra draws on Shiva's tapa to regenerate himself.

The practice of igniting tapa is known as tapasya. It involves not responding to any worldly stimuli. He who performs tapasya and churns the fire of tapa is known as a Tapasvin. A Tapasvin's eyes are always shut. He does not see the world. He does not even feel the world. Hence serpents and creepers can wind round his limbs and termites can build hills round his flesh.

Shiva is the supreme Tapasvin, still and unmoving as the mountain he sits on. There is so much tapa in Shiva's body that water does not flow around him; it freezes to become snow. Shiva's abode, the snow-capped Kailasa, is unfit for habitation.

It cannot support life. Daksha therefore does not like Shiva. He finds no point in offering any of his daughters to Shiva. He prefers offering them to the Devas. Empowered by the chants and offerings of the yagna, the Devas are able to rotate the wheel of samsara, overpower the Asuras, draw and distribute rasa, and bring rain, children and harvests, to the delight of Daksha.

Yagna empowers the Devas but not the Asuras. The Asuras therefore turn to tapasya in their quest for power. Through

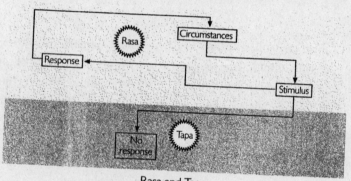

Rasa and Tapa

Table   Representations of Rasa and Tapa

Rasa	Tapa
Open eyes	Shut eyes
Flowing river	Still mountain
Sex	Celibacy
Red and green	White
Water	Fire
Sandal paste	Ash
Woman	Man
Melody	Silence
Downward flow of semen	Upward flow of semen
Downward-pointing triangle	Upward-pointing triangle

ascetic practices they invoke God and obtain boons. With these boons they defeat the Devas, and withdraw rasa back into their subterranean realms. In the following narrative, Shukra, guru of the Asuras, is able to obtain from Shiva the science of resurrecting the dead.

Shukra

Empowered by Vedic chants, the Devas could easily kill the Asuras. Not knowing what to do, Shukra, guru of the Asuras, performed tapasya. By lighting the inner fire of tapas, he hoped to overpower the outer fire favouring the gods. He hung himself upside down from the branch of a tree over a raging fire, breathing nothing but smoke for a thousand years. When these austerities reached their climax, Shukra came face to face with Shiva. Shiva opened his mouth and swallowed Shukra, trapping him within his body. Shukra tried to escape but found that Shiva had closed all his orifices, all except the penile passage. As Shukra slipped out of this aperture, he came to possess all the knowledge that enabled him to resurrect the Asuras killed by the Devas in battle. This was Sanjivani Vidya. (Mahabharata)

In the natural world, dead are reborn, not resurrected. But with tapa it is possible to subvert natural laws, resurrect the dead, walk on water, fly in the air, change the size and shape of any creature, manoeuvre the course of destiny and fulfil any desire. When the

Asuras use the power of tapa to outwit death, the Devas seek the help of God or Goddess to restore the order of samsara.

Raktabija

Raktabija invoked Brahma and sought from him the boon of immortality. When that was not forthcoming he asked that whenever a drop of his blood fell on earth another Raktabija would spring up. Thus, he would never die. The world would be full of his duplicates. The Devas dared not attack Raktabija. No sooner did their weapons strike him than his blood fell to the ground and more Raktabijas came into being. Terrified, the Devas invoked the Goddess, who took the form of Kali and spread her tongue over the earth and drank every drop of the Asura's blood before it touched the ground. No new Raktabija sprang up. Drained of every drop of blood, Raktabija toppled lifeless. (Kalika Purana)

The power to subvert natural law through tapa is known as siddhi. When a Tapasvin acquires siddhi, he becomes known as a Siddha. Any jiva—even a human—can become a Siddha if he can overpower the urge to respond to sensory stimuli. Once a Siddha, a human becomes more powerful than a Deva, capable of doing whatever he wills.

A Siddha must be differentiated from a Rishi. A Rishi obtains his power from the Devas by chanting the appropriate hymns and making the appropriate offerings during yagna. Siddhas bypass the Devas and go directly to God to get their powers. In the following story, the Rishi Vasistha gets his magical cow from the Devas. Envious of this, Kaushika practises tapasya, intent on obtaining magical powers that will make him more powerful than not only the Rishis but also the Devas.

Kaushika and Trishanku

A king called Kaushika once paid a visit to the hermitage of a Rishi known as Vasistha. He was accompanied by his soldiers. Though the king's arrival came as a surprise, Vasistha was able to provide him and all his entourage a sumptuous meal, thanks to Kamadhenu, a magical cow gifted to him by the gods. Kaushika felt that such a cow deserved to be with a king and decided to claim the cow by force, much to Vasistha's dismay. However, when his soldiers approached the cow, the cow gave birth to warriors who were able to drive Kaushika and his soldiers away. This magic so impressed Kaushika that he lost all interest in his kingdom. Royal power was nothing compared to the power of magic. So he decided to pursue tapasya. He gave up his crown and went to the forest to become a Tapasvin. During his absence, there was a famine in the kingdom. His family starved. They would have died of starvation had a man called Trishanku not fed them some meat. Unknown to them, this meat was of a cow. No other vegetable or meat was available during the famine. Indebted to Trishanku for saving his family, Kaushika offered him a boon. Trishanku said, 'Help me enter Swarga.'

Using the power of all the tapa he had accumulated, Kaushika caused Trishanku to rise above the earth. Trishanku rose higher and higher but, when he reached the gates of Swarga, he was stopped by Indra, king of the Devas. 'This man is an adulterer, a cow-killer and a beef-eater. He is unfit to reside among the gods.' Indra pushed Trishanku down towards the earth. However, Kaushika was determined to keep his end of the bargain. He prevented Trishanku from landing on the ground. Trishanku remained suspended head downwards between the sky and the earth. Kaushika then used his power of tapa to create a new Swarga where Trishanku could live, neither on the ground nor above the ground, but somewhere in between.
(Kurma Purana)

That Kaushika abandons his wife and children to become a Siddha shows that to churn tapa one must refrain from conjugal relations. Rishis, like Daksha, on the other hand, offer their daughters to the Devas and encourage conjugal relations. Celibacy retains all reproductive juices within the body and ignites tapa. Sex releases reproductive juices out of the body and ensures the flow of rasa.

According to Tantra, only men have the biology to ignite tapa and acquire siddhi. While all other creatures can suspend the workings of sense and action organs, only the human male has control over his reproductive organs. Plants, animals and women shed their seed during pollination, heat and menstruation whether they want to or not. Hence they cannot retain rasa. Unfettered by the cycles of nature, a man can restrain his sexual urges, retain rasa, ignite tapa and acquire siddhi.

Mahadevi

The Goddess is often shown placing her foot on human heads or wearing a garland of human heads. The heads are invariably male and moustachioed. The male moustachioed head represents the ego. The ego seeks validation and approval from the external world. It seeks to control the external world to ensure this validation and approval. This quest for validation, approval and control stems from a failure to understand the world is the Goddess—infinite and impermanent—existing to direct the mind towards the divine within, God, formless, nameless, permanent. While the jiva is on a journey of self-discovery, Mahadevi nurtures it with her fertility. But when the jiva attempts to control her fertility in the pursuit of self-actualization, she strikes it down violently.

The Devas are wary of Siddhas because they have the power to disrupt the balance of nature that the Devas struggle to maintain. They therefore do everything in their power to arouse sexual desires and disrupt tapasya. Indra, king of the Devas, is always on the lookout for women abandoned by their husbands. His unabashed carnality exasperates ascetics and sages who struggle to discipline their sexual desires.

Ahalya

While the sage Gautama was away, Indra seduced Gautama's wife, Ahalya. As they were making love the sage returned. Enraged, he turned his wife into stone. He castrated Indra and caused his body to be covered with a thousand vaginas. (Ramayana)

According to Tantra, seed can flow in two ways. Downwards and outwards to produce new life. Upward and inwards to ignite tapa. The latter reverse flow of semen is the goal of a Tapasvin. The Devas enlist the help of Apsaras to prevent Tapasvins from reaching this goal.

Apsaras are nymphs well versed in the sixty-four ways to satisfy the senses. Apsa means water in Sanskrit. An Apsara is thus a water-nymph who has to douse the flames of tapa. She embodies rasa just as a Tapasvin embodies tapa. She is the outer worldly life. He is the inner spiritual life. She enchants. He struggles against her enchantments. She wins when the Tapasvin sheds semen and embraces worldly life.

Menaka

Indra, king of the gods, sent a nymph called Menaka to seduce Kaushika. Menaka danced before Kaushika until he was forced to open his eyes and submit to her charms. Together, Kaushika and Menaka produced a child. Thus did Menaka succeed in destroying the tapasya of Kaushika. No more did he threaten the workings of the world. He became a friend of the world, hence was renamed Vishwamitra. (Mahabharata)

But no Apsara can make Shiva open his eyes or spill his semen. For Shiva has destroyed Kama, desire itself, by the blaze of his tapa.

Burning of Kama

Kama was asked by the gods to enchant Shiva. Kama's presence filled the air with romance: Shiva's snow-capped mountain transformed into a pleasure garden full of flowers, bees and butterflies. Flowers bloomed to greet Kama; they made offerings of pollen and nectar at his feet. Apsaras danced while Gandharvas sang, cheering Kama, who raised his sugar cane bow, drew his bowstring of bees and shot five arrows at Shiva. The arrows stirred Shiva's senses. He was not amused. He opened his third eye and let loose a fiery missile that set Kama ablaze and reduced him to ashes. Having destroyed the lord of sensory indulgence, the lord of sensory discipline resumed his meditation. (Shiva Purana)

Shiva's tapa leaps out of his third eye. This eye stands vertical and is oriented neither to the left nor to the right. At no point does Shiva open his left or right eye. These eyes represent conventional standards and values. Shiva's third eye transcends all standards and values; it looks beyond. And so Shiva does not distinguish between beauty and ugliness. Nothing attracts or repels him. He feels no desire. He is indifferent to all things worldly; hence Kama has no power over him.

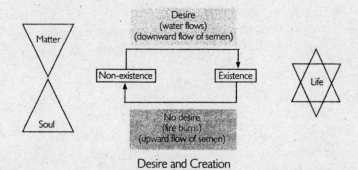

Desire and Creation

Shiva may be the lord of Siddhas, the supreme Tapasvin, but he has no desire to subvert the workings of nature. Unlike Kaushika or the Asuras, he has no interest in the outer world. His attention is inward. He seeks not siddhi, power over things worldly, but samadhi, freedom from all things worldly. Shiva uses the flames of tapa to burn all memories, desires, ideas, values and standards that crumple his chitta. In the light of the fire Shiva sees the true nature of the world around, hence the true nature of the self within. With true knowledge of Pursuha and Prakriti, Shiva feels no urge to act or react. He experiences bliss, ananda. This ananda causes his phallus to rise.

In the following story, Rishis misinterpret Shiva's erect phallus. They think he is aroused by the enchantments of the

material world. They fail to notice that, though Shiva's manhood
is aroused, his eyes are shut. The stimulus is not external but
internal. The erect phallus, the linga, is self-stirred, a result of
spiritual enlightenment. The erect phallus of Shiva represents
the inner flames of tapa. It is the symbol of ananda, true bliss
that follows the uncrumpling of the mind.

Enlightenment through Dance

A group of Rishis was performing yagna in a forest when
Shiva passed by. Shiva was naked, his phallus erect. The
wives of the Rishis were aroused by Shiva. Losing all
interest in the yagna, they pursued Shiva. This angered
the Rishis. They used the power of yagna to create a tiger,
a venomous snake and a demon. Shiva flayed the tiger
alive, and wrapped the skin around him. He caught the
snake and wound it round his neck like a necklace. Then,
leaping on the demon's back, he began to dance. As he
danced, the sages realized Shiva was God and his dance
was a visual discourse on the true purpose of existence—
not to indulge the ego and change the world but to
discover the divine within with the help of the divine
without. (Skanda Purana)

Shiva is not just a Tapasvin. He is also a Yogi. The aim of yoga is to
unknot the mind, uncrumple the consciousness, attain the triple
state of sat–chitta–ananda: unconditional truth, purified

consciousness, tranquil bliss. Shiva is therefore associated with bilva leaves, whose three leaves represent sat–chitta–ananda and whose stalk holding the three leaves together represents yoga. The three blades of Shiva's trident also represent sat–chitta–ananda and its staff represents yoga.

Nataraja

Shiva communicates the truth of life through dance. Dance is the symbol of life. It is impermanent, lasting as long as the dancer dances. It flows through space and time, unfettered by any dimension or moment. The wheel around the dancing Shiva is the merry-go-round of worldly events. The ego is swept away by the wheel. Shiva crushes the ego and dances on its back, offering an alternative. He balances himself on his right foot, indicative of the still Purusha, and swings his left leg, indicative of the ever-changing Prakriti. His right hand comforts his devotees while his left hand points to the interaction of the left and right feet. The fire he holds in one hand is tapa, ignited by refusing to submit to worldly stimuli. The rattle-drum in the other is created with the downward-pointing triangle of matter separated from the upward-pointing triangle of the spirit.

Shiva's sacred mark is three horizontal lines made of ash. The three lines represent the three worlds and the three bodies. When they are burned by the fire of tapa, ash is produced. Ash is the symbol of the soul. Like the soul it is indestructible. Like the soul it is released only when matter is destroyed by fire. The horizontal orientation of Shiva's sacred lines represents inertia. Shiva is the complete opposite of Vishnu, whose sacred mark is oriented vertically, indicating activity. Shiva withdraws from the world to contemplate on it. Vishnu participates in the world to celebrate it. Shiva's passivity is fit for hermits. Vishnu's active gaze is sought by householders.

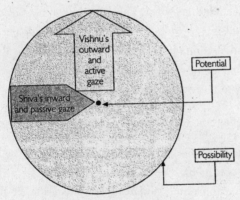

Shiva's Way and Vishnu's Way

Determined to break free from all things worldly, Shiva cuts the fifth head of Brahma—the ego—which makes Brahma lose his identity, identify himself with the outer world and chase his own daughter in passionate, incestuous pursuit. Shiva uses the fifth head of Brahma as his begging bowl, hence is known as Kapalin, the skull-bearer.

Brahma's Fifth Head

After Brahma created his daughter, she went around him
as a mark of respect. Enchanted by her beauty, Brahma
sprouted four heads, facing the four cardinal directions,
so that he could look upon her at all times. When she flew
skywards, he popped a fifth head on top of the other four.
This display of unbridled passion disgusted the daughter.
She cried. In response, Shiva appeared in a terrifying form
and wrenched off the fifth head of Brahma. (Shiva Purana)

In Shiva's hand is a deer. The deer is the symbol of the mind
because it is as restless as the mind. Shiva stills the deer that is
the mind by pinning it down with the bow of yoga.

Shiva, the Archer

Brahma began chasing his daughter. She took various forms
of birds and beasts. For every form she took, he took the
form of the male complement. When she became a cow,
he became a bull. When she became a doe, he became a
buck. The daughter cried out. Immediately, Shiva raised
his bow and shot an arrow at Brahma, pinning him down.
(Linga Purana)

Shiva, the fountainhead of yoga, is associated with all things that
never die and never change. He sits atop a mountain, under a

banyan tree, located under the Pole Star, in the north. He is called Dakshina-murti because he looks towards the south. South is the direction ruled by Yama, god of death, destiny and change. It is associated with movement, with rasa, with the Goddess.

Dakshina-murti

Shiva sits facing the south, revealing the secret of tapasya, the art of igniting fire that can prevent the waters of samsara from overwhelming one's mind. North, home of the still Pole Star, is where Shiva sits unflustered by the rhythms of rasa. He sits under the banyan tree, symbol of permanence.

It is from the south that the Goddess approaches as Dakshina-Kali, dark and terrifying, naked, soaked in blood, covered with corpses. She is the embodiment of raw and untamed nature. Her nakedness draws attention to nature's sexuality that creates life; her fangs and bloodshot eyes, a reminder of nature's violence that destroys life. This sex and violence establish the cycle of creation and destruction and rotate the wheel of samsara, ensuring the preservation and propagation of all living creatures. She is the ever-changing, fertile world Shiva has shut himself from.

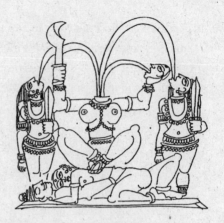

Chinnamastika

Chinnamastika is a Tantrik goddess who embodies rasa, the juice of life. A new life is created only when rasa flows during sex. A life is sustained only when rasa is consumed as food. To produce food, rasa from another life has to be claimed. By sitting on top of her lover, Prakriti is forcing Purusha to partake of life and thus create new life. By cutting her own head and drinking her blood, Prakriti reminds Purusha that no life can be sustained without consumption of another life. Rasa is what makes the world go round. Tantra is alchemy, the art of making the juice or rasa move in a desired direction.

It is desire that links Purusha with Prakriti. It is desire that will make Dakshina-murti open his eyes to Dakshina-Kali. The Goddess is determined to evoke desire in Shiva's eyes. This will never happen so long as the third eye is open. For love to happen, the third eye must close and the left and right eyes must open.

From Kailasa to Kashi

In this section we see that the restlessness of matter validates itself as being necessary in the search for stillness.

Daksha and Shiva, the Rishi and the Yogi, embody two opposing approaches to life. For the Rishi, the world is Shakti, energy with the power to make existence delightful. For the Yogi, the world is Maya, delusion. Truth lies beyond the enchanting forms created by space, time and matter. From the Rishis came Vastu-shatra, Jyotisha-shastra and Ayur-veda, sciences that aim to manipulate space, time and body to harness happiness, fortune and health. Shiva being the ascetic has no interest in happiness, fortune or health. Space, time and body do not interest him. He therefore prefers the inner fire to the outer fire. His doctrine is yoga, the science of managing the mind, uncrumpling the consciousness and attaining sat–chitta–ananda.

Table   Difference between Yagna and Yoga

Yagna	Yoga
Documented in the 'Brahmana' scriptures	Documented in the 'Aranyaka' scriptures
Seeks to appease gods	Seeks God within
Vedic mantras are chanted	Vedic mantras are contemplated upon
Outward looking	Inward looking
Involves rituals	Involves austerities
Seeks to change the world	Seeks to change perception of the world
Popular among householders	Popular among hermits
Aligned to social structures such as caste	Rejects social structures
Involves lighting an outer fire	Involves lighting an inner fire
Can be performed only with wife	Must be practised alone
World affirming	World renouncing

Daksha and Shiva steer clear of each other. Daksha does not offer Shiva any of his daughters. Shiva is not interested in marrying anyone anyway. The Goddess takes birth as Sati, Daksha's youngest daughter, and from a very young age expresses her desire to marry Shiva. Daksha shows no interest in having Shiva for a son-in-law, while Shiva shows no interest in having Sati for a wife. Despite the lack of encouragement, Sati is determined to bring Daksha and Shiva together.

Sati embodies the voice of those who challenge ritualism because it gives more importance to the mechanical execution of ceremonies than to the needs of the heart and the questions of the mind. Shiva's intellectual detachment from things worldly is not the answer either. Sati yearns for the middle path where there is husband's love and father's affection. She begins by turning away from Daskha and following Shiva, making no demands, loving him unconditionally, so much so that Sati comes to mean 'the ideal wife'. Despite her determined efforts, nothing changes. Shiva refuses to open his eyes and embrace her. Finding Shiva as continent as ever, Daksha finds no value in inviting him to his yagna. Stranded between her father's stubborn adherence to the demands of formal ritual and her husband's indifference, Sati takes a decision to stir passion in both their hearts.

Daksha Insults Shiva

Sati once saw that the gods and their wives were on their way to her father's yagna. She decided to go there too. 'Why?' asked Shiva. 'Because he is my father, and daughters don't need invitations to visit their father,' replied Sati.

Shiva shut his eyes but let his wife go. When Sati reached her father's house, she found all the gods gathered to receive the offerings of the yagna. There was no seat reserved for Shiva. She realized her father had deliberately not extended an invitation to her lord. 'He does not know how to dress or behave in public. He covers himself with ash. Holds a skull in his hand. Lives in crematoriums with ghosts and dogs for company. Does not even show me the respect due to a father-in-law. This makes him unworthy of any offering,' said Daksha. Sati was upset and angry. In her fury, she leaped into the sacred fire of the yagna, determined to pollute the sacred fire and stop the ritual. Agni, the fire-god, refused to touch her. So Sati invoked tapa, the inner fire, and set herself alight on the sacred altar. With that the sacred precinct was polluted and Daksha's yagna ground to a halt. (Kalika Purana)

The death of Sati sets the stage for a violent confrontation between the world-rejecting Shiva and the world-affirming Daksha. News of Sati's demise stirs emotions Shiva has never experienced before. There is loss, pain and rage. The fire withheld in his body for centuries explodes like a volcano, taking the form of Virabhadra.

Destruction of Daksha's Yagna

Sati's death broke Shiva's heart. His serenity was shattered. He was furious. In his rage, he pulled out his hair and created a fanged warrior called Virabhadra. Virabhadra rushed into Daksha's house, followed by hordes of ghosts and goblins who rode on rabid dogs. The air was

filled with the howl of death. The followers of Shiva leaped
on the assembled Devas, ripping out their hearts and
gouging out their eyes. They drank blood and bedecked
themselves with limbs and entrails. Virabhadra caught
Daksha hiding behind the altar. With one swoop of his
axe, he beheaded the great patriarch and tossed his head
in the altar. (Linga Purana)

Sati brings Shiva in touch with his feelings. In her company he
experiences love. In her absence, he experiences sorrow. Her
death makes him realize the cruelty of social rules and regulations
that often ignore feelings in the quest to establish order. His
outrage manifests itself through his followers, the gana, who
spread mayhem wherever they go. By destroying the yagna, they
destroy society with all its values and judgements.

Virabhadra

Virabhadra is a violent form of Shiva associated with outrage and punishment.
He is associated with dogs and ghosts. In his hand he holds the head identified

either as Brahma or as Daksha. Virabhadra is the alter ego of the serene Shiva who meditates on Kailasa. For many, Virabhadra is the warrior manifestation of Shiva to be invoked before battle. Others see Virabhadra as Bhairava, the fear-evoking form of Shiva.

But the rage and retribution, the destruction of society, do not take away the pain. Shiva clung to Sati's corpse and wandered across the three worlds, howling in agony. His tears turned into sacred beads known as Rudraksha, meaning 'from the eyes of Rudra who is Shiva'. The beads thus represent the reaction of Shiva when he finally came in touch with samsara.

Restoration of Daksha's Yagna

After destroying Daksha's sacrifice and bringing death and destruction to the sacred precinct, Shiva picked up the charred remains of Sati's body and wandered around the world, howling in agony. The world had become a miserable place, full of suffering. Vishnu was alarmed. He feared for the well-being of the cosmos. So he raised his serrated discus that destroys all negativity and hurled it in the air. It cut Sati's body into 108 pieces. With the body gone, Shiva regained his senses. He restored the gods to life and revived Daksha by replacing his severed head with that of a goat. Daksha completed his yagna and empowered the Devas so that the cycle of life could rotate once more. This time an offering was made to Shiva too, at the end of the ritual. Shiva let his dogs consume it. He simply withdrew into a cave, shut his eyes and immersed himself in his inner world, where

he relit the fire of tapa and destroyed his ties with the
outer world. (Vishnu Purana)

Vishnu can understand Shiva's rage against the nature of
civilization, but he cannot let Shiva destroy society. By destroying
Sati's corpse, he is able to make Shiva detach himself from the
stimulus of pain. With Sati gone, Shiva is able to overcome his
grief and sense of loss. He can even let go of his outrage. He
resurrects Daksha by replacing his head with that of a goat and
lets him continue as before as patriarch of the Vedic civilization.

Shiva, however, remains an outsider. He disengages himself
from the world, seeking freedom from those stimuli that cause
pain and suffering. Sitting atop Mount Kailasa, he shuts his eyes,
withdraws his senses inwards, relights the fire of tapa and lets
his phallus stir in self-containment.

As Sati, the Goddess makes Shiva experience bhoga, the
pleasure of the senses and the joy of emotions. But these sensory
pleasures and emotional joys have a rhythm—waves and troughs;
pleasure is followed by pain, joy by sorrow, just as day is followed
by night, summer by winter, high tide by low tide. Shiva discovers
this in his moment of crisis. He responds by recoiling from the
world. He withdraws from all senses and detaches himself from
all emotions. He uses yoga to prevent his mind from being swept
away by samsara. A mind swept away by the ever-changing
material world ends up being controlled by memories, desires,
ideas and ego. It therefore experiences suffering, pain, misery,
frustration, anxiety and insecurity. With tapa, Shiva destroys

memories, desires, ideas and ego. With yoga he uncrumples his consciousness. There is no confusion then. Only clarity.

Yoga is essentially a technique of mental discipline used to still the mind and manage a crisis. There are different types of yoga for different types of people: bhakti yoga for those who are more emotional, gyan yoga for those who are more intellectual, karma yoga for those who are more social, hatha yoga for the athletic, mantra and tantra yoga for those more ritualistic. Though different in form, the underlying principle in each is the same— to burn reactions of former actions without generating new actions that entrap one in samsara. Whatever the type of yoga chosen, the ultimate destination is sat—chitta—ananda.

Table Different Types of Yoga

Type of Yoga	Means for Mental (Cosmic) Control
Bhakti	Humility and devotion
Gyan	Intellectual activity
Hatha	Physical austerities
Karma	Detached participation in worldly affairs
Tantra (Laya)	Rituals
Mantra (Japa)	Hymns and chants

Traditionally, yoga has been divided into the approach of Shiva and the approach of Vishnu. Shiva's approach is more inward looking, ascetic and intellectual, while Vishnu's way is more outward looking, emotional and social. The former tends to be more world rejecting and the latter tends to be more world affirming. Shiva's path is the path of the hermit, nivritti marga. Vishnu's path is the path of the householder, pravritti marga.

Bhagavad Gita

Through the song of God, Krishna communicates the wisdom of yoga to Arjuna just before the Mahabharata war. Krishna represents the realized soul, free of all conditioning, capable of seeing the truth as it is. He is the self in a state of sat–chitta–ananda. Arjuna is consciousness crumpled by conditioning. The chariot he rides is the body. The horses are his senses. The two wheels are the two forces of the cosmos: kama and karma, desire and fate. As charioteer, Krishna does two things: he helps Arjuna realize the true nature of life and at the same time overpowers the forces that threaten social order.

Vishnu seeks to balance material aspirations with spiritual goals. He integrates yoga with bhoga. He proposes dividing life into four stages: the first involving preparing for material life, the second involving enjoying material life, the third involving renunciation of material life and the fourth involving total focus on spiritual goals.

As Krishna, Vishnu proposes an alternative that allows for simultaneous rather than sequential achievement of material joy and spiritual bliss. He classifies all actions into two: reaction and response. In the former, one is guided by one's ego, motivated by one's desires. In the latter, one is guided by one's intellect, motivated by one's duty. The former focuses on result. The latter focuses on action. By responding rather than reacting, by maintaining equanimity and not getting provoked by worldly stimuli, it is possible to satisfy the demands of worldliness, fulfil one's obligations to society, repay one's debts to ancestors and still attain moksha.

Table Shiva and Vishnu

Shiva	Vishnu
Sits on snow-capped mountains and caves	Reclines on ocean of milk or in meadows and palaces
Smeared with ash; wears animal skins, beads and skulls	Anointed with sandal paste; wears silk, gold and flowers
Eyes shut and lips serene	Eyes open and lips curled in a smile
Associated with dogs, ghosts and bulls	Associated with cows, women and horses
Destroys Kama	Kama is the son of Vishnu and Lakshmi
Beheads Brahma	Gives birth to Brahma
Has to be forced into marriage	Enjoys the company of wives and lovers

In art, hooded serpents or Nagas are used to represent both bhoga and yoga. The Goddess holds a slithering serpent in her hand. Shiva has a Naga coiled round his neck, its hood expanded in wisdom. Only when a serpent slithers can it shed skin. The slithering, mobile serpent therefore represents bhoga, the waxing and waning material pleasures that please the senses. Only when the serpent is still and coiled can it open its hood and look at the world. The coiled serpent with expanded hood represents yoga. The slithering serpent represents the flowing rasa. The coiled serpent is the blazing tapa. Movement is thus associated with fertility and pleasure; stillness with serenity and sterility. Vishnu is associated with both the slithering serpent and the coiled serpent. As Krishna he dances on the slithering serpent; as Narayana he sleeps on the coiled serpent. The coiled serpent is like snow, frozen water. The slithering serpent is the life-giving river. The coiled serpent is like raw milk, full of potential. The slithering serpent is like butter, the realization of milk's full potential.

Table Representations of Yoga and Bhoga

Yoga	Bhoga
Sensory discipline	Sensory indulgence
Stillness	Movement
Snow	River
Water	Fire
Man	Woman
Hermit	Householder
Raw milk	Butter
Seeds	Flowers
Coiled serpent	Slithering serpent
White	Red

Vishnu constantly strives to balance yoga and bhoga. He has therefore beside him Saraswati, embodiment of yoga, dressed in white, and Lakshmi, embodiment of bhoga, dressed in red. Shiva stays clear of bhoga, all things worldly.

In Tantrik geometry, the downward-pointing triangle represents Prakriti while the upward-pointing triangle represents Purusha. Brahma causes the two to intersect, creating a six-pointed star that spins around Vishnu's finger as the Sudarshan chakra. Shiva separates the two triangles to create his rattle-drum. The star-discus represents engagement of spiritual and material reality that gives rise to the world of name and form. The rattle-drum represents the separation of spiritual and material reality resulting in the nameless, formless unmanifest. While pursuing the common goal of sat–chitta–ananda, God as Vishnu preserves the realm of rasa while God as Shiva destroys the realm of rasa in the flames of tapa.

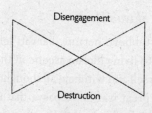

The Rattle-drum of Shiva and the Discus of Vishnu

The Goddess does not accept Shiva's total withdrawal. Stillness may be serene but it is also sterile. A banyan tree may offer shade and hold the promise of permanence, but it does not let even a blade of grass grow around it, nor does it provide life-sustaining fruit for man. The banana plant offers no shade but its rapid regenerative ability ensures it provides food to sustain the family. Snow may be still but cannot sustain life. To sustain life, it must melt, turn into a river and flow down the plains.

And so, like the flowing river and the regenerating banana plant, like everything material and impermanent, the Goddess returns. Having died as Sati, she is reborn as Parvati, princess of the mountains. Again determined to marry Shiva. Again wanting to shatter his tranquil isolation with the turbulence of rasa.

That the Goddess is Himavati, the daughter of the snow-capped mountain Himavan, is significant. The mountain represents tapa, stability, stillness. By emerging from it, she informs Shiva that tapa and rasa are in essence the same. Just as he retains rasa to ignite the flame of tapa, she intends to use the flame of tapa to restore the flow of rasa.

Parvati Wins Shiva's Heart

Determined to marry the stubborn hermit, Parvati left her father's house and took to living like an ascetic in the forest. She withdrew into herself and withheld all thought, action, breath and seed. So great was her tapasya that it shook the mountain on which Shiva sat. His serenity shattered, he was forced to open his eyes and appear before Parvati. He tried to dissuade Parvati—informing her that life with a hermit would be nothing like the life she had with her royal father. He suggested she marry a prince or a god, someone young and handsome and virile. But Parvati would not budge. She was determined. Shiva was forced to acknowledge that he had met his match. He agreed to marry Parvati. (Shiva Purana)

The Goddess makes the impossible possible through determination. She makes Shiva, destroyer of Kama, open his eyes and fall in love. This narrative draws attention to the power of determination. Determination is an expression of desire. Through determined expression of desire it is possible to change destiny. This principle forms the foundation of the ritual practice known as vrata, followed in most Hindu households.

During vrata, determination is expressed in many ritually prescribed ways such as fasting, staying awake all night, eating particular kinds of food and avoiding others, visiting particular shrines or invoking particular deities at regular intervals for prolonged periods of time. For example, a woman may visit a Shiva shrine every Monday for sixteen weeks, eating and drinking nothing all day in the hope of getting a good husband. Vrata is commonly associated with 'sympathetic or imitative magic'. The object of desire is integrated into the ritual in symbolic form. Those who seek permanence, to cope with the insecurity of life, visit a banyan tree or a shrine under it during vrata. Those who seek wealth and prosperity surround themselves with sugar cane, honey, butter, coconuts, mangoes, bananas, rice, gold and perfumes. Vratas are not concerned with lofty spiritual goals like moksha. They are concerned with ordinary household material aspirations: marriage, children, health and prosperity.

While the Goddess appreciates the value of yoga, she does not let Shiva pursue it at the cost of worldly life. For her, the simple household joys matter. Bent on making a householder of this hermit, she insists Shiva marry her in the ritually prescribed manner. But Shiva does not know how. He has knowledge of the truth. But he has no knowledge of maya, the conditional truths of culture that give rise to rules and regulations, rituals and responsibilities. Indifferent to worldly ways, the great god,

Mahadeva, who is God, makes a fool of himself as he tries his best to become Parvati's groom.

The Hideous Groom

Parvati told Shiva that he must come to her house with his family on the wedding day and ask from her father her hand in marriage. Shiva had no family; so he invited his companions to his wedding. To the horror of the gods, the retinue comprised ghosts, goblins, gnomes, witches, vampires and dwarfs. Shiva himself rode a bull. He smoked hemp and drank poison. His companions, innocent of worldly ways, bedecked him with whatever they could find: ash, skulls, bones, serpents and animal hide. When he arrived at the gates of the mountain-god's palace, the women who had assembled to welcome him ran away scared. Mena, Parvati's mother, refused to accept this man who looked like a beggar and resided in crematoriums as her son-in-law. Parvati pleaded with Shiva, 'You promised to marry me. So take the form that pleases my parents at least until they have given me away as your bride.' So Shiva let the gods bedeck him as they deemed fit. Shiva was bathed with celestial waters and adorned with silks, flowers, gold and gems. When the gods were finished, he looked more handsome than Kama himself. He was as fair as the full moon. His limbs were lithe like those of a dancer. All the assembled women fell in love with him. They declared him Sundareshwara, the lord of beauty. Even Mena was impressed. With joy she let Shiva marry her daughter. In the presence of the gods, in a ceremony presided over by Brahma himself, Shiva and Parvati exchanged garlands to become husband and wife. (Shiva Purana)

Parvati soon discovers that the third eye that enables her husband to overpower Kama prevents him from acknowledging social norms that separate right from wrong, the appropriate from the inappropriate. In his eyes, all things are manifestations of matter, equally pure and impure. There is no divide between the auspicious and the inauspicious. Life in the crematorium is as sacred as life on a ritual altar where yagna is performed. The culturally constructed difference between mother and wife which makes no sense in the natural world makes no sense to Shiva's third eye either. This is made explicit in the following story.

Killer of Andhaka

Parvati, in a spirit of play, covered Shiva's left and right eyes. Instantly the world plunged into darkness because Shiva's eyes were the sun and the moon. To save the world, Shiva opened his third eye and put light back in the world. But the heat of the third eye caused Parvati to perspire. From this perspiration, there came a child who was called Andhaka, born of darkness, because he was born when Shiva's left and right eyes were covered. Shiva gave Andhaka to the demon-king Hiranayaksha, who was childless. Andhaka was raised among the demons and he eventually became king of the demons. Andhaka

performed tapasya and obtained from Brahma a boon—
that he would be killed only if he looked upon his mother
with lustful eyes. Andhaka believed this was not possible
as he had no mother. Andhaka soon led the demon
armies and overpowered the gods. He became ruler of
the three worlds. A time came when he decided his vast
kingdom needed a queen. He decided to make the most
beautiful woman in the three worlds his wife. He was
informed that none was more beautiful than Parvati, the
mountain-princess, who had given up the comforts of
her father's palace to be the wife of the hermit Shiva.
Andhaka immediately proceeded to Shiva's abode,
determined to make Parvati his wife. He offered Parvati
gifts and promises of love. Parvati was not amused. She
turned away. So Andhaka decided to take her by force.
'Help me, my lord,' cried Parvati when Andhaka's
attentions became unbearable. Shiva appeared on the
scene, impaled Andhaka with his trident and let his blood
flow out until he was reduced to nothing but a bag of
bones. Impaled on Shiva's trident for aeons, Andhaka
realized he was the child of Shiva and Parvati. He begged
for forgiveness and sang songs to the glory of the divine
couple. (Vamana Purana)

Shiva is not ignorant of worldly ways. He is simply innocent of
them. He is therefore Bholenath, the guileless one. In Tantrik texts,
it is the Goddess who initiates Shiva into the erotic arts. Shiva
follows her teachings. But he is so guileless that he does not know
when to exercise restraint or demonstrate modesty.

Trapped in Yoni

The sage Bhrigu once went to Mount Kailasa intent on offering obeisance to Shiva and Shakti. He found Shakti on top of Shiva, making love. The intrusion embarrassed the Goddess, who covered her face with a lotus. Shiva, however, continued copulating. Bhrigu realized Shiva would not stop because in his innocence he had no sense of shame. Bhrigu decided to worship Shiva and Shakti symbolically as a linga enveloped by a yoni. (Linga Purana)

Linga Shrine

Linga means phallus. Yoni means the womb. A Shiva temple, and by extension the whole world, is the yoni of the Goddess. The entrance to the yoni is the leaf-shaped trough within the temple, which envelops Shiva's linga. The Goddess thus draws Shiva's phallus into the world. The tip of the leaf-shaped trough always points to the north, suggesting that Shiva is lying on the ground facing the south while the Goddess is sitting on top facing the north. That the Goddess is always visualized as sitting on top of Shiva is indicative of her proactive role in making Shiva interact with the world. This highly erotic imagery is typical of Tantra. It seeks to shock one into enlightenment. Tantrik scriptures describe Shiva as shava or corpse, totally indifferent to external stimuli, yet sporting an erect phallus stirred by the inner realization of sat–chitta–ananda. The Goddess hopes to transform this shava into Shiva by enveloping the self-stirred svayambhu linga with her yoni. Water is poured on the symbol of Shiva and collected in the symbol of Shakti with the aim of drawing the energy of Shiva's fire into samsara.

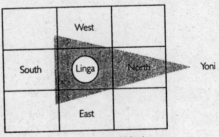

Linga and Yoni

The marriage of Shiva and Shakti transforms both God and Goddess. When she steps on Shiva, Shakti is Kali, nature wild and untamed. Shiva is consciousness that is indifferent. When they marry, Kali becomes Gauri, nature that is nurturing and fertile. Shiva becomes Shankara, consciousness that is attentive. Just as devotees pour water on Shiva to draw his attention towards them, they offer clothes to Shakti when they visit her shrine. They want to see her not as the naked and bloodthirsty Kali but as the maternal Gauri.

Kamakshi

The Goddess is associated with all the symbols of Kama, including sugar cane, flower arrows and parrots. She sits on Shiva and forces him to participate in worldly life. He faces the south; she faces the north. He faces the impermanence of the world, the ever-flowing rasa. She faces the permanence of the soul, the ever-blazing tapa.

Kali and Gauri

To help the Devas, the Goddess once took the form of Kali and killed all the Asuras. But then she continued drinking blood, and indulged in an orgy of violence, scaring the Devas, who turned to Shiva for help. To stop the Goddess, Shiva threw himself on her path. Kali stepped on him. Embarrassed that she had stepped on her husband, she bit her lip. That is why Kali has her tongue outstretched. She decided to shed her dark form. She dipped in the river Yamuna and emerged as Gauri, bright and radiant. (Bengali Folkore)

Kali and Gauri are the untamed and domestic forms of the Goddess. One is naked, the other fully dressed. One's hair is unbound. The other's is tied with a string of flowers. The form that is Durga stands in between, reconciling the two extreme forms. In Durga sex and violence are disciplined enough to become protective and nourishing but not totally domesticated. Hence, like Kali, and unlike Gauri, Durga's hair is unbound. But like Gauri, and unlike Kali, Durga is fully dressed.

Table The Metaphorical Use of Hair

Type of Hair	Meaning
Unbound hair	Untamed senses
Tied hair	Tamed senses
Matted hair	Absolutely controlled senses
Plaited hair	Young virgin
Parted hair	Deflowered woman
Unshaved head	Householder
Partially shaved head	Part-hermit, part-householder
Fully shaved head	Hermit

When Shakti draws Shiva's heat, the snows of Kailasa melt and a river is born. It flows south, fertilizing the plains. The river is the most perfect symbol of samsara and the Goddess. It is never still. One can never step into the same river twice. It slips out of clenched fists. But it gives life, sustains civilization.

Gangadhara

When the Devas send the river-nymph Ganga to flood the earth, Shiva entraps her in the matted locks of his hair. She is the embodiment of rasa that can overwhelm the senses. Shiva's matted hair represents the total mental discipline of yoga that can prevent this from happening. Had the Goddess not been by his side, Shiva would have frozen the river, turned it into snow. But instead, he releases it slowly so that it flows gently, sustaining life on her banks. Thus the energy withdrawn by tapasya is released through the taming of Ganga. Tapa is transformed to rasa, which then sustains the world.

The following story shows the interdependence of impermanence and fertility. Worldly life may not be still, but it is its changing form that allows for harvests.

Annapurna

Shiva once told Shakti that he was tired of her many forms: the wild Kali, the gentle Gauri, the protective Durga. He did not see any value in these forms. So she disappeared.

In her absence there was no one to provide Shiva food. Hungry, Shiva could not meditate or contemplate. He was forced to leave Kailasa and go to the plains, where people lived, and beg for food. But wherever he went he found no food. The hunger pangs drove him mad. Finally, he learned that Shakti had taken up residence in Kashi and that anyone who entered her kitchen was given food. Shiva rushed there with his bowl and begged Shakti to feed him. She did. His hunger satisfied, Shiva acknowledged the importance of Shakti. He named her Annapurna, granter of food, and refused to let her go. (Kashi Mahatmya)

In Kailasa, Shiva lives in serene isolation. But in Kashi, he lives with his wife as Shankara, the benevolent one, granter of boons. In the snow-clad mountain, he may be the distant ascetic. In the riverside city, he is the householder.

A Head for Ganesha

In this section the conflict between matter and soul, the divine without and the divine within, is resolved.

Although Brahma chases the Goddess and Vishnu protects the Goddess, it is Shiva—the destroyer, the reluctant groom—who is the father of her children. Within the temple, Shiva may be a formless symbol, an aniconic linga enveloped by a yoni. But on temple walls and in calendar art, he is part of a family portrait complete with his wife and his sons. The children of God and Goddess represent the perfect balance of spiritual pursuits and material aspirations that makes life worthwhile.

Shiva's Family

Shiva, with the domesticated form of the Goddess, represents consciousness that is not indifferent, but attentive, to worldly matters. This form of Shiva is called Shankara. The result is children who balance spiritual bliss with material delight. The warrior Kartikeya represents brawn and temporal power. The corpulent Ganesha represents brain and worldly prosperity.

A son fathered by Shiva, the Devas believe, will be strong enough to lead them to victory in their battles against the Asuras provided he is incubated outside Shakti's womb. According to Tantrik physiology, a child is conceived when the white seed of man successfully fuses with the red seed of woman. The child is male when the white seed is more powerful, female when the red is more powerful and hermaphrodite when both seeds are equally powerful. Since Shiva and Shakti are equally matched, the gods fear Shiva's seed incubated in Shakti's womb may turn out to be a hermaphrodite, with all his masculine traits neutralized by all her feminine traits. So they do everything in their power to prevent Shiva's seed from entering the womb of the Goddess.

The child ends up being nurtured in several wombs—that of fire, wind, water and earth. The child thus born of Shiva's seed and nurtured in several wombs is called Skanda, a spurt of blazing tapa. He becomes the warlord of the gods, supreme commander of celestial armies.

Birth of Skanda

Taraka, an Asura, had obtained a boon from Brahma that he could be killed only by a warrior who was six days old. The Devas realized that such a warrior could only be fathered by Shiva. For Shiva's semen, unshed for aeons, blazed with the power of tapa. A child born of it would be hypermasculine and virile enough to ride into battle on the seventh day of its life. So they interrupted the love-making of Shiva and Parvati. Embarrassed, Parvati turned away and Shiva's semen spurted out. The fire-god Agni caught the semen in his flames but found its radiance too powerful to bear. To cool it down, he gave the seed to Vayu, the wind-god, who—having failed in this endeavour—plunged it into the icy waters of the river Ganga. The river water started to boil, such was the energy contained in Shiva's seed. Six forest-virgins, the Krittikas, wives of six of the seven celestial sages, who were bathing in the river became pregnant with that one seed. Their husbands declared them unchaste. In shame, they cleared their wombs and abandoned the unborn fetuses in the care of Saravana, the forest of reeds. No sooner had the fetuses touched the ground than the forest of reeds was set ablaze. In the forest fire the six fetuses united to become one child with six heads. The Krittikas wanted to kill this child as he embodied their shame. But as soon as they came near him, their breasts started oozing milk. Overcome by maternal affection the Krittikas nursed this child, whom they named Kartikeya, the son of the Krittikas. The child born of Shiva's seed that had been drawn by Parvati and incubated by Agni, Vayu, Ganga and Saravana, and nursed by the Krittikas was also named Skanda. On the seventh day of his life, Skanda was strong enough to pick up a lance and lead the gods into battle against Taraka. After a fierce fight he triumphed over Taraka. (Skanda Purana)

Skanda is truly a hypermasculine being capable of going to war when he is but six days old. By defeating Taraka, Skanda helps the Devas draw out rasa from beneath the earth's surface. Thus, through Skanda, Shiva participates in worldly affairs.

Murugan–Kartikeya–Skanda

In art, Skanda is represented by symbols of masculinity such as the lance, the rooster and the peacock. He is associated with the planet Mars. Skanda is popularly worshipped in South India as Murugan, the boy-god, and as Kumara, the eternal child. He is Subrahmaniam, the helpful god, who stands atop mountains and protects mankind. He has two consorts: Sena, the daughter of the Devas, and Valli, the daughter of local tribes. According to some, his wives are symbols of his army and his weapons to which he is married. In North India, he has no consorts. He is a virile warmonger who takes men to battle and makes widows of women.

In many narratives, the role of the Goddess is taken up by Vishnu's female form known as Mohini. Mohini means the one who enchants. Like the Goddess, Vishnu seeks to enchant Shiva into worldly life. By taking advantage of Shiva's innocence, Vishnu makes the fire-churning ascetic shed his semen. From this semen are born warrior-gods such as Ayyanar and Manikantha.

Embracing Mohini

Vishnu once took a female form, that of the enchantress Mohini. Such was her beauty that even Shiva was enchanted. He embraced her and spilt his semen. From that semen was born Manikantha, the son of Shiva and Mohini. Manikantha was given to a childless Chera king and grew up to be a great ascetic-warrior. After his adoption, his foster mother bore a son. Determined to secure the throne for her own son, the queen feigned illness and begged Manikantha to fetch her the milk of a tigress which alone, the doctors claimed, could cure her. Manikantha went to the forest, overpowered many demons and returned with the milk of a tigress. He gave up his claim to the throne so as to truly 'cure' his mother. He chose instead to live as a celibate ascetic atop a hill overlooking his father's kingdom. (Sabarimala Sthala Purana)

Manikantha, also known as Ayyappa, is a popular god in Kerala. In images he is shown squatting with cloth tied just below his knees. Local lore has it that his father, the king, tied him thus to prevent him from running away from the world. He thus stays atop the hill known as Sabarimala, protecting and providing for all those who come to him.

Hanuman is another warrior-god born of Shiva's semen shed at the sight of Mohini. Like Manikantha, he is also celibate, shying away from women and worldly life. Hanuman derives his strength from his celibacy. The retained semen transforms into tapa, energizing his mind and body, making him as sharp as lightning and as strong as thunder. Unlike an ordinary Tapasvin who uses the power of tapa, that is siddhi, for personal gain, Hanuman uses his siddhi to help those who come to him. He can change the planetary positions and change the destiny of people. He is the force of yoga that will overpower the ego personified in Ravana and unite Sita, the jiva-atma, with Rama, the param-atma.

Hanuman

Hanuman is the mighty monkey-god of the Hindus who is renowned for his humility, celibacy and strength. Monkeys represent the restless mind. By devoting himself to Rama, who is God incarnate, a monkey overpowers the natural instincts of sex and violence to become Hanuman. His kaupina or loincloth indicates his chastity and restraint. This generates tapa and gives him the power to carry mountains and destroy the ego. His orange-red colour represents the tapa he embodies; his tail a reminder of his potent power, resulting from devotion and discipline.

Skanda, Ayyappa and Hanuman may be children born of Shiva's semen but the Goddess is not satisfied with them. They do not represent Shiva's direct interest in worldly affairs. They are not produced consciously and willfully. The shedding of semen is unintentional, almost accidental. The fact remains that his marriage is forced and their love-making, with her on top, is one-sided. The Goddess wants more of Shiva. She wants a more conscious, proactive, participation. And so she demands that Shiva make her a mother.

Birth of Ganesha

Parvati wanted Shiva to father a child. But he refused. An exasperated Parvati created a child on her own, using the turmeric paste with which she had anointed herself. The child was called Vinayaka because he was born without the intervention of a man. Parvati asked her son to guard the entrance to her bath and not let anyone in. Vinayaka obeyed, blocking even Shiva's entry, not knowing he was his mother's consort. An otherwise detached Shiva lost his cool, raised his trident and beheaded the stubborn lad. Parvati was inconsolable in her grief and threatened to transform from Gauri, the life-giving goddess, to Kali, the life-taking goddess, if her son was not resurrected. Shiva therefore ordered his followers, the ganas, to fetch him the head of the first living being they encountered. They brought back the head of an elephant, which Shiva placed on the severed neck of Parvati's son and restored him to life. By giving him life, Shiva became the boy's father. He acknowledged his fatherhood by naming the lad Ganapati, lord of the ganas. (Shiva Purana)

Vinayaka stirs emotions of jealousy in Shiva, and provokes him into violence. The action leads to reaction, a series of events which culminates in the beheading of the child. Parvati's fury at the death of her child forces Shiva to act. When he resurrects her creation and appoints him leader of his followers, he consciously becomes father and thus part of the material world. The resurrected Ganapati with a body created by the Goddess and a head given by God represents the transformation of Shiva the hermit into Shiva the householder.

If Kartikeya is the warrior son of Shiva, Ganesha is the scholar son. Kartikeya is born of Shiva's seed while Ganesha is born of Parvati's body. Kartikeya is associated with fire, Ganesha with water. Kartikeya is tapa. Ganesha is rasa. Through these two sons of Shiva and Shakti, the grace of God and Goddess reaches humanity.

Table   Kartikeya and Ganesha

Kartikeya	Ganesha
Muscular and virile	Fat and fertile
Associated with masculine symbols like ash, lance, peacock and rooster	Associated with feminine symbols like water, elephant, serpents and banana plant
Warrior	Scholar
Married to his army and his weapons	Married to wealth and wisdom
Commander of the Devas	Scribe of Rishis

The choice of an elephant's head for Ganesha is interesting. In Hindu symbolism, the elephant is the symbol of material abundance. Indra, king of the gods, rides an elephant. Elephants flank Lakshmi, the goddess of wealth and prosperity. Shiva, who rejects material pleasures, is described as Gajantaka—he who flays the elephant and uses its thick skin as his upper garment. By using the elephant's head to resurrect the child of his consort, Shiva in effect demonstrates his participation in the world of rasa. He uses the power of tapa to bring to life the child he killed.

Ganapati's head represents tapa; his body represents rasa. He reconciles God and Goddess. He becomes the doorway through which Shiva enters samsara.

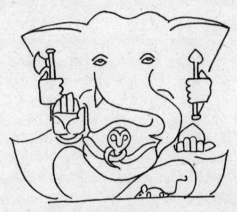

Ganesha

Ganesha has an elephant's head, a corpulent body and a serpent tied round his stomach. Elephant, pot belly and serpent are material symbols. That the upper part of his body is created by Shiva and the lower part by Shakti makes him a liminal deity who brings together God and Goddess, soul and substance, spiritual bliss and material delights. Ganesha is the lord of thresholds, sitting between yoga and bhoga, discipline and indulgence, monastic orders and fertility rites, Vedic speculation and Tantrik rituals. In some scriptures, Riddhi and Siddhi, wealth and wisdom, are his wives. Subha and Labha, auspiciousness and profit, are his sons. Santoshi, satisfaction, is his daughter. His rat represents the unmanageable, stubborn problems of life that he keeps at bay. Ganesha is thus the god of the present, sitting between the past and the future, removing all obstacles, ensuring the realization of every dream.

With a child in her arms, the Goddess is no more the terrifying Kali. She is Gauri, the mother. In Maharashtra, following the rains,

Gauri, dressed in green, is worshipped along with Ganesha. Green is the colour of vegetation, motherhood, fulfilled desires. Gauri represents fulfilled desires, the fructification of earth's fertility. She is the domesticated form of the Goddess. Her hair is tied in a bun with a string of flowers.

Later in the year, around the time of the autumn harvest, the Goddess is worshipped dressed in red with hair unbound. In this form known as Durga, she is a warrior, riding into battle on a lion, holding weapons in her hand. In Bengal, this form is associated with gods and goddesses who are described as her children. They include two daughters, Lakshmi and Saraswati, and two sons, Ganesha and Kartikeya. Thus, the children of the Goddess embody wealth and knowledge, brain and brawn. They are born only when Shiva, consciousness, becomes her husband and stops being indifferent.

Finally, just before winter, is the festival when the Goddess takes her most sexual and violent form, that of Kali. In this form she is no longer the milk-giving mother. She is the bloodthirsty killer. In this form she demands replenishment of her energy. Blood and milk, like water and sexual fluids, are forms of rasa. By drinking blood she is able to provide milk for her children.

When winter gives way to spring, the Goddess once more becomes the virginal bride of Shiva. The marriage of Shiva and Parvati is celebrated on the night known as Maha-Shiva-ratri. A fortnight later, the death and resurrection of Kama is celebrated during Holi, a festival of colours when men and women throw water on each other to soothe burning passions. Thus through a cycle of festivals, the Goddess ensures the participation of Shiva in the wheel of samsara.

Table   The Three Forms of Shakti

Gauri	Durga	Kali
Dressed in green	Dressed in red	Naked
Maternal	Bridal	Carnal
Hair bound	Hair unbound	Hair dishevelled
Associated with a cow	Rides a lion	Rides a lion
Vegetarian	Accepts all offerings of devotees	Demands blood sacrifice
Wears symbols of marriage	Wears bridal jewellery	Covered with entrails and human heads
Holds no weapons	Holds weapons in a defensive stance	Holds weapons in an offensive stance
Offers food	Does not offer food	Does not offer food

Ganesha is the first lord according to Tantra. Tantra seeks the truth through the Goddess; hence it is known as Vama-marga, the female path, to be contrasted with Dakshina-patha, the male path of Vedanta, which seeks the truth through God. In Tantra, truth is realized in phases. Each phase involves the uncrumpling of consciousness and the blooming of a flower or chakra. The first flower to bloom is Muladhara. Ganesha is lord of this first chakra. Since the participation of Shiva is necessary to create Ganesha, the first flower of Tantra blooms only after the first contact with Shiva, the realization that life is not just the outer ever-changing world perceived by the senses; there is more, within, unchanging and still, beyond the reach of the senses.

As the journey of self-realization progresses and the uncrumpling of chitta continues, more flowers bloom, each with its own deity. Thus according to Tantra, gods and goddesses are manifestations of the consciousness, helping us discover the truth about ourselves and our world. The final chakra blooms above

Table The Seven Chakras of Tantra

Location of Chakra	Name of Chakra	Phase of Self-discovery
Crown	Sahashrapadma	Self-realization
Brow	Agna	Self-reflection
Throat	Vishuddha	Self-expression
Heart	Anahata	Self-acceptance
Navel	Manipura	Self-definition
Genitals	Svadhisthana	Self-gratification
Anus	Muladhara	Self-preservation

the head. It is described as a thousand-petalled lotus within which is a jewel. That lotus is in its fullest manifestation. The jewel is Purusha in its perfection. The jewel in the lotus is thus a metaphor for world-realization, self-realization, truth-realization. Like the erect phallus of Shiva, the dreamless slumber of Vishnu, it symbolizes sat–chitta–ananda. The difference here is God's eyes are open. He is fully aware of the Goddess.

The Tantrik approach to self-realization is different from the Vedic approach. The former looks upon the Goddess as Shakti, energy, to be experienced while the latter looks upon the Goddess as Maya, delusion, to be transcended. The former is therefore more sensory, the latter less so. That is why Tantrik images are vivid, erotic and intensely colourful. In Tantra, the world is experienced to the fullest, shattering all cultural norms; hence Tantrik texts unashamedly prescribe unsocial activities. The aim is to get as close to nature as possible, shattering the tyranny of cultural values and judgements. In the Vedic approach, self-realization has to be achieved by detached adherence to cultural values and judgements, social roles and ritual conduct. Or it has to involve total distancing from sex and violence through practices such as vegetarianism, fasting and non-violence. Both approaches ultimately aim to understand the truth of the Goddess and through her the truth of God. As householder or hermit, the truth must be realized.

God can be either a hermit or a householder. Shiva's sons Ayyappa and Hanuman are hermits. Ayyappa's shrine is not visited by women. And Hanuman is worshipped by householders only because he is visualized as the son of the Goddess, her doorkeeper, with his sexual and violent urges controlled by yoga. The form of Kartikeya that is worshipped is always the one which is associated with wives or the one where he is an innocent child. People avoid temples of Kartikeya where he is a bachelor. It is as if Kartikeya becomes worthy of worship when his sexual energy is absent or contained through marriage.

Although Shaiva lore takes great pains to describe the marriage of Shiva, they never clarify the marital status of Ganesha and Kartikeya. Some say Ganesha is a bachelor. Others say he has two wives. Some say Kartikeya is a bachelor. Others say he has two wives. In North India, Kartikeya is not worshipped by women because he is unmarried. In South India, where he is worshipped, he has two wives. In shrines, Ganesha is always associated with Lakshmi and Saraswati. Some say these are his sisters. Some say these are his wives, forms of Riddhi and Siddhi. Once again, it is association with Goddesses that makes the deity complete, worthy of worship.

Likewise, while the raw power of the Goddess is greatly admired, when she is worshipped there is an insistence to see her either as mother, with her children, or as a bride, wearing a nose-ring and bangles. Just as marriage makes the indifferent God attentive, marriage makes the wild Goddess nurturing.

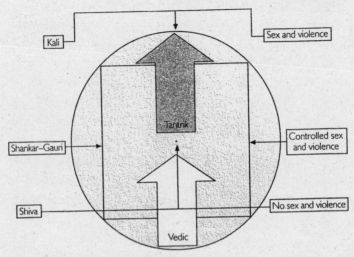

Shiva–Kali versus Shankar–Gauri

The marriage of God and Goddess, the need to complete divinity through both male and female forms, the urge to introduce a square between the circle and the point, draws attention to the eternal conflict in the Hindu psyche between the permanent soul and the impermanent world. What matters more: the mundane world of space and time or the transcendental realities that are dimensionless and timeless? Does worldliness justify existence? Or is the world with its conditional truths and transient values to be shunned, outgrown, in the quest for something greater, more permanent and absolute?

Marriage is a metaphor for worldliness, the union of soul and flesh. When God marries, he becomes part of the world. When God refuses to marry, he stays away from the world.

Why should God be part of the world? Why should God not be part of the world? Who is God? Why does the world matter so much? Why does the world exist? Is participation in worldly affairs the only validation of existence? But what is existence? What exists truly—the constantly changing world, the restless mind or the still, serene soul? Who is this person reading this book? Who is this person writing this book? The mind? The soul? The world?

Is he, or she, Brahma, so passionate about life that he/she has totally identified him/herself with the outside world, losing all sense of self? Is he, or she, Vishnu, with a well-ordered, regulated, enjoyable yet detached relationship with the world? Or is he, or she, Shiva, so sensitive to the meaningless uncertainties and unending transformations of life that he or she yearns to withdraw to a solitary space where there is stillness and peace?

Perhaps he, or she, is Indra still waiting to realize that the world is not limited by his or her vision and vocabulary.

A Palace for Indra

Indra, god of the sky, king of the Devas, once asked his architect, Vishwakarma, to build him a palace befitting his stature. 'For I am the overseer and lord of the three worlds,' he said. Vishwakarma built him a magnificent palace of crystal surrounded by lakes and gardens. But this did not please Indra. 'This is good,' said the ruler of the skies, 'but not good enough. Build me something grander befitting my stature. For I am the overseer and lord of the three worlds.' So Vishwakarma built another palace. More magnificent than the one before. Even this did not please Indra. 'No, no. Something even grander befitting my stature. For I am the overseer and lord of the

three worlds,' said Indra. An exasperated Vishwakarma
went to his father, Brahma, for help. Brahma invoked
Vishnu, who took the form of a boy and presented himself
before Indra. Indra welcomed his guest and asked him
the purpose of his visit. 'To see if your palace is better
than the palace of the other Indras,' answered the boy.
'Other Indras? What do you mean "other Indras"?' Indra
asked, perplexed. The boy replied, 'The other Indras.
Those who existed before you. Those who will come after
you. And those who exist right now in parallel worlds.
There have been countless Indras in the past. There will
be countless Indras in the future. And there are countless
Indras in the present. You are but one grain of sand in a
beach of Indras. Each and every Indra rules the sky and is
a king of the Devas. Each one wants his Vishwakarma to
build him a grand palace befitting his stature. I have visited
them all.' Humbled by this information, Indra stopped
making his palace grander. (Brahmavaivarta Purana)

Hindu seers long ago realized the world is limitless and boundless,
full of unimaginable potential and possibilities. Any attempt to
fathom its mystery through science, mathematics and logic was
futile. What mattered more than the objective world was the
subjective world of each individual. Hindu seers therefore
focused their attention and genius less on geography and history
and more on philosophy and metaphysics. What mattered more
than the landscape of the world was the landscape of the soul.

The seers wondered why the world is as diverse as it is.
Why does it sometimes bring fortune and then, inexplicably,

misfortune? Why does it favour some and not everyone? Why is it so affectionate sometimes and ruthless at other times? Why does it simultaneously give joy and sorrow? Why does it at once frighten and fascinate? What is the reason behind it all?

Perhaps our world is the mirror of our soul. It is the source and destination of all our memories, our desires, our ideas, our feelings, our thoughts, our values and our judgements. It exists because we are aware of it. We know we exist because we are aware of it. Our world cannot exist without us. We cannot exist without our world. Without either there is neither. We are inextricably bound to each other. Our life is a life-long affair with our world that will end when we die. All meaning that we seek has to lie somewhere beween us and our world. There is no one else between the two of us.

Ardhanareshwara

Shiva as half woman represents the union of God and Goddess, the divine inside and the divine outside. In this form there is no split between the individual and the world, the self and the non-self, the subject and the object, the seer and the scenery. God and Goddess split and separate when the soul seeks to know itself. The journey begins with the quest to possess the world, continues with the quest to organize and appreciate the world and ends with a true understanding of the world. With world-realization comes self-realization. Goddess-realization leads to God-realization. When this happens, the divide between the self and the other ceases to be. There is union. Dissolution.

As we explore and experience of worldly life, as we meet our destiny and realize our desires, our vision and vocabulary will expand. With it will expand our world. We will discover that the world outside is as limitless and boundless as the self within. Containing everything and nothing simultaneously.

Inside are Brahma, Vishnu and Shiva, creating, sustaining and destroying. Outside are Saraswati, Lakshmi and Shakti, enlightening, enriching and empowering. Around us are the goddesses. Within are the gods.

God and Goddess.
Purusha and Prakriti.
Observer and observation.
Subject and object.

That's what it is. Not this, not that; this too, that too.
That's who we are.
Tat tvam asi.

Glossary of Non-English Words

ananda	bliss, tranquillity, serenity
Apsara	water-nymph, celestial dancer
ashrama	stage in life
Asura	subterranean being who hoards wealth
atma	soul
avatar	incarnation
bhakti	passionate devotion
bhoga	sensory indulgence
chitta	consciousness, spirit, mind
daan	charity
dakshina	service fee
Deva	celestial being who draws and distributes wealth
devata	personal deity
dharma	order, regulations
Gandharva	celestial musicians
jiva	living organism
jiva-atma	soul of a living organism that is crumpled/knotted
kalpa	lifetime of the world
kama	desire
karma	action and reaction
manas	mind
Manava	human
mantra	potent Vedic chants
marga	path or approach
maya	delusion; a limited, conditional understanding of the world

mithya	relative truth seen through a frame of reference
moksha	liberation
murti	image
nivritti	inward
param-atma	soul of god that is uncrumpled/unknotted
Prakriti	ever-changing aspect of life, mind and matter
pravritti	outward
puja	adoration or worship of a deity with flowers, incense and food
Purusha	unchanging aspect of life, soul
Rakshasa	wild forest spirit who follows the law of the jungle
rasa	material fluids
Rishi	sage with a deep understanding of Vedic lore
samadhi	using spiritual powers to break free from the world
samaja	society
samhita	collection of chants
samsara	the material world that changes constantly
samskara	rite of passage
sat	absolute truth without a frame of reference
shakti	energy, matter
shanti	peace
sharira	body
siddhi	the act of using spiritual powers to change the working of the world
Tantra	occult practices based on Vedic understanding of the world
tapa	spiritual fire
Tapasvin	an ascetic who churns spiritual fire
tapasya	practices that churn spiritual fire
tat tvam asi	that's what you are
tirtha	pilgrimage to a waterbody: river or lake or tank

Upanishad	deliberations and discussions on the Veda
varna	station in society
Veda	ancient revelations containing timeless truths
yagna	invocation of celestial beings through chants and offerings in fire
Yaksha	wild forest spirit who guards treasures
yantra	potent Tantrik diagrams
yatra	journey
yoga	sensory discipline
Yogi	he who practises yoga
yuga	an era in the lifetime of the world

Bibliography

Abbot, J.E. and N.R. Godbole. *Stories of Indian Saints*. Delhi: Motilal Banarsidass, 1996.

Bhattacharji, Sukumari. *The Indian Theogony*. New Delhi: Penguin Books, 2000.

Coupe, Lawrence. *Myth*. London: Routledge, 1997.

Dange, Sadashiv Ambadas. *Encyclopaedia of Puranic Beliefs and Practices*, Vols 1–5. New Delhi: Navrang, 1990.

Danielou, Alain. *Gods of Love and Ecstasy: The Traditions of Shiva and Dionysus*. Rochester, Vt.: Inner Traditions International, 1992.

_____. *Hindu Polytheism*. Rochester, Vt.: Inner Traditions International, 1991.

Eliade, Mircea. *Myths, Dreams, and Mysteries*. London: Collins, 1974.

Flood, Gavin. *An Introduction to Hinduism*. New Delhi: Cambridge University Press, 1998.

Frawley, David. *From the River of Heaven*. Delhi: Motilal Banarsidass, 1992.

Graves, Robert. *The Greek Myths*. London: Penguin Books, 1960.

Hawley, J.S. and D.M. Wulff, eds. *The Divine Consort*. Boston: Beacon Press, 1982.

Highwater, Jamake. *Myth and Sexuality*. New York: Meridian, 1990.

Hiltebeitel, Alf, ed. *Criminal Gods and Demon Devotees*. New York: State University of New York Press, 1989.

Hiltebeitel, Alf. *Cult of Draupadi*, Vol. 1. Chicago: University of Chicago Press, 1988.

Hopkins, E. Washburn. *Epic Mythology*. Delhi: Motilal Banarsidass, 1986.

Jakimowicz-Shah, Marta. *Metamorphosis of Indian Gods*. Calcutta: Seagull Books, 1988.

Jayakar, Pupul. *The Earth Mother*. Delhi: Penguin Books, 1989.

Jordan, Michael. *Myths of the World*. London: Cambridge University Press, 1993.

Kinsley, David. *Hindu Goddesses*. Delhi: Motilal Banarsidass, 1987.

Klostermaier, Klaus K. *Hinduism: A Short History*. Oxford: Oneworld Publications, 2000.

Knappert, Jan. *An Encyclopedia of Myth and Legend: Indian Mythology*. New Delhi: HarperCollins, 1992.

Kosambi, Damodar Dharmanand. *Myth and Reality*. Mumbai: Popular Prakashan Pvt. Ltd, 1994.

Kramrisch, Stella. *The Presence of Shiva*. New Delhi: Motilal Banarsidass, 1988.

Mani, Vettam. *Puranic Encyclopaedia*. Delhi: Motilal Banarsidass, 1996.

Martin-Dubost, Paul. *Ganesha: Enchanter of the Three Worlds*. Mumbai: Franco-Indian Research, 1997.

Mazumdar, Subash. *Who Is Who in the Mahabharata*. Mumbai: Bharatiya Vidya Bhavan, 1988.

Meyer, Johann Jakob. *Sexual Life in Ancient India*. Delhi: Motilal Banarsidass, 1989.

O'Flaherty, Wendy Doniger, trans. *The Rig Veda: An Anthology*. New Delhi: Penguin Books, 1994.

———. *Origins of Evil in Hindu Mythology*. New Delhi: Motilal Banarsidass, 1988.

———. *Hindu Myths*. Delhi: Penguin Books, 1975.

O'Flaherty, Wendy Doniger. *Sexual Metaphors and Animal Symbols in Indian Mythology*. New Delhi: Motilal Banarsidass, 1981.

———. *Siva: The Erotic Ascetic*. London: Oxford University Press Paperbacks, 1981.

Panati, Charles. *Sacred Origins of Profound Things*. New York: Arkana, 1996.

Pandey, Rajbali. *Hindu Samskaras*. Delhi: Motilal Banarsidass, 1969.

Pattanaik, Devdutt. *Indian Mythology: Tales, Symbols and Rituals from the Heart of the Indian Subcontinent*. Rochester, Vt.: Inner Traditions International, 2003.

_____. *Lakshmi, Goddess of Wealth and Fortune: An Introduction*. Mumbai: Vakil, Feffer and Simons, 2003.

_____. *Hanuman: An Introduction*. Mumbai: Vakil, Feffer and Simons, 2001.

_____. *Man Who Was a Woman and Other Queer Tales from Hindu Lore*. New York: Harrington Park Press, 2001.

_____. *Devi: An Introduction*. Mumbai: Vakil, Feffer and Simons, 2000.

_____. *Goddess in India: Five Faces of the Eternal Feminine*. Rochester, Vt.: Inner Traditions International, 2000.

_____. *Vishnu: An Introduction*. Mumbai: Vakil, Feffer and Simons, 1999.

_____. *Shiva: An Introduction*. Mumbai: Vakil, Feffer and Simons, 1997.

Sen, Makhan Lal. *The Ramayana of Valmiki*. Delhi: Munshiram Manoharlal, 1978.

Subramaniam, Kamala. *Srimad Bhagavatam*. Mumbai: Bharatiya Vidya Bhavan, 1987.

Walker, Benjamin. *Hindu World*, Vols 1 and 2. Delhi: Munshiram Manoharlal, 1983.

Wilkins, W.J. *Hindu Mythology*. Delhi: Rupa, 1997.

Zimmer, Heinrich. *Myths and Symbols in Indian Art and Civilization*. Delhi: Motilal Banarsidass, 1990.

Index

Available from Penguin
THE BEST-SELLING GODS AND GODDESSES SERIES

The lives of gods, goddesses and prophets
retold for the modern reader
through fascinating interpretations of myths, rituals,
scriptures and iconographic representations
in simple, accessible language